Significant differences

Critical Psychology

Series editors

John Broughton
Columbia University

David Ingleby
Vakgroep Ontwikkeling en Socialisatie, Utrecht

Valerie Walkerdine
University of London Institute of Education

Since the 1960s there has been widespread disaffection with traditional approaches in psychology, and talk of a 'crisis' has been endemic. At the same time, psychology has encountered influential contemporary movements such as feminism, neo-marxism, post-structuralism, and post-modernism. In this climate, various forms of 'critical psychology' have developed vigorously.

Unfortunately, such work — drawing as it does on unfamiliar intellectual traditions — is often difficult to assimilate. The aim of the Critical Psychology series is to make this exciting new body of work readily accessible to students and teachers of psychology, as well as presenting the more psychological aspects of this work to a wider social scientific audience. Specially commissioned works from leading critical writers will demonstrate the relevance of their new approaches to a wide range of current social issues.

Titles in the series include

The Crisis in Modern Social Psychology
Ian Parker

The Psychology of the Female Body
Jane M. Ussher

Significant Differences
Corinne Squire

Significant differences

Feminism in psychology

Corinne Squire

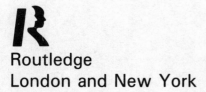

Routledge
London and New York

First published 1989
by Routledge
11 New Fetter Lane, London EC4P 4EE
29 West 35th Street, New York, NY 10001

© 1989 Corinne Squire

Phototypeset in 10pt Times by
Mews Photosetting, Beckenham, Kent
Printed and bound in Great Britain by
Biddles Ltd, Guildford and King's Lynn

British Library Cataloguing in Publication Data

Squire, Corinne, *1958–* .
  Significant differences: Feminism in
  psychology — (Critical psychology
  series)
  1. Psychology related to feminism
  2. Feminism related to psychology
  I. Title II. Series
  150

Library of Congress Cataloging in Publication Data

Squire, Corinne, 1958–
    Significant differences: feminism in psychology / Corinne Squire.
      p. cm. — (Critical psychology series)
    Bibliography: p.
    1. Women — Psychology. 2. Feminism — Psychological aspects.
  3. Psychology. 4. Feminist criticism. I. Title. II. Series.
  HQ1206.S69   1989
  155.6'33 — dc19   88-13828
                                                              CIP

ISBN 0-415-01224-4
ISBN 0-415-01225-2 (pbk)

Contents

Acknowledgements

Participants at the 1986 Cardiff Women in Psychology and the 1987 Manchester Psychology Politics Resistance conferences provided useful suggestions about early versions of parts of this book. Pam Calder, Ron Moule and John Munford made valuable comments on draft chapters. John Broughton and David Ingleby gave me some very helpful advice about what to leave out and put in. Valerie Walkerdine's patient and detailed criticisms of successive drafts were invaluable. I benefited a lot from discussions with Iraina Clarke, Barbara Khwaja, and Pat O'Neill, about the general direction of the book. I am also grateful to Neil Turok for his careful, encouraging criticisms at various stages of the writing.

Introduction

Psychology as a scientific discipline should develop and take seriously its awareness of the unfortunate and unwarranted consequences of reproducing and maintaining oppressive gender-belief systems, if a non-sexist discipline is to develop.

(Burns and de Jong 1986: 1)

The psychological bondage remains even after its economic rationale has dissolved.

(Rowbotham 1973: 80)

Feminism and psychology are important for each other. Their inter-dependence shows up in a variety of historical and social contexts. Nineteenth- and early twentieth-century feminists often cited psycho-logical studies of the power of social learning, and drew radical implications for women from psychoanalytic ideas. Some psychoanalysts and psychologists endorsed early feminist demands, and this occasional support has continued. Within contemporary psychology, gender issues are a widespread focus of interest. Sex roles and sex stereotyping are an important topic of psychological research in South and Central America, for example (Ramirez 1985, Rodrigues 1985). Many contem-porary feminists are, in turn, concerned with psychological issues, and feminists in developing countries are especially interested in social psychological analyses of women's roles.

Current western feminism and psychology seem to have a particu-larly close relationship. Feminism devotes itself primarily to studying and trying to change gender relations; psychology takes individual subjectivity as its main object of investigation. But postwar, second-wave western feminism has come to see an understanding of the complexities and contradictions of subjectivity as a precondition for changing gender relations. At the same time, western psychology is increasingly realizing that the gender relations which feminists study influence many aspects of subjectivity. Feminism could learn from the detailed, persistent attention psychology gives to subjectivity. Mainstream psychology, which consistently underplays the importance of social relations and disdains theory, could learn a lot from feminist work in these areas. And so sharing the insights of feminism and psychology could be helpful to both. But they have yet to establish a productive relationship.

In the 1960s and early 1970s, feminists often wrote off subjective experiences of gender as false consciousness. Subsequently, they have been more likely to make these experiences the central feature of gender relations: 'the relationship of man to woman is like no other relationship of oppressor to oppressed. It is far more delicate, far more complex. After all, very often the two love each other' (Rowbotham 1973: 33–4). Feminists have paid little explicit attention to psychology as a discipline, except to censure its patriarchal aspects. They display a critical fascination with psychoanalysis, a field many psychologists do not even consider part of the discipline. Despite, and partly because of, this selective neglect, feminists have developed much more sophisticated accounts of gendered subjectivity than have mainstream psychologists.

Feminists sometimes treat subjectivity reductively, and find it difficult to connect psychological issues to workable politics. But they usually pay subjectivity some attention. Psychology, on the other hand, frequently ignores gender issues altogether. Alternatively, it marginalizes them within the specialized areas of the psychology of women, or of sex differences. Even here, it tends to deal with them in a prejudiced, slipshod, or unsystematic way. Psychology has responded to feminist criticisms of such failings with a much greater intolerance and neglect than that shown by disciplines like sociology, history, and literary studies. At best, it asserts its scientific disinterestedness, and declares its freedom from pro- or anti-feminist interests. Influential members of the British Psychological Society, for example, feared that initial proposers of a Psychology of Women Section were trying, 'under the guise of a scientific Section . . . to become the kind of pressure group that the Society cannot formally accommodate'. They argued that members should instead 'be ensuring that equal opportunities exist throughout the whole Society' (Newman 1985).

Psychology is a discourse, a structure of knowledge and power.[1] This structure is constituted by and in turn helps to determine social relations. However impartial it claims to be, it affects and is affected by gender relations. Psychology's partial awareness of this has prompted a few concessions to feminism. Some psychologists argue for more women psychologists, more work on women and sex differences, and more methods and theories which address common female as well as male experiences. But psychology still deals with feminism on its own terms. It tries to fit feminist arguments into its own, scientific, discursive structure, and it tends to give up on them if this proves difficult.

Feminism has had wider influences on psychology than the discipline recognizes. It has encouraged investigations of female-identified aspects of psychology, like parenting and the emotions, among male as well as female psychological subjects. It has contributed to psychology's awareness of the unconscious, of language, and of historical and social relations. It has intensified interest in non-experimental, qualitative procedures, and in more representative and diverse design. And it has stimulated theoretical concern with balancing biological and cognitive with social explanations, with interdisciplinary work, and with analysing psychology's own epistemological and political nature. But psychology's reluctance to acknowledge the radicalism of feminist arguments makes it very difficult to develop wide-ranging, persistent and effective feminist psychological initiatives.

Some of the problems feminist psychologies encounter come from feminism, as well as from traditional psychology. Both feminism and psychology deploy a concept of a unitary, rational subject. This concept tends to channel them towards asocial, ahistorical and psychological analyses. Within feminist psychology, the concept often allows gender, a variable cultural structure (Oakley 1972), to be reduced to the fixity of biological sex.[2] As a result, feminist psychologies often assume that a female subject is either just like a male subject, or completely different from him. They tend to treat all women and all men as if they were the same; to ignore the complexity and extent of the power relations which affect subjects; and to replicate the stasis and dogmatism of traditional psychology.

This book describes contemporary feminist psychological initiatives, the difficulties they encounter, and the productive tactics they develop: tactics which allow them to address both the subjective experiences and the power relations of gender, and in the process to change the nature of psychological discourse. Feminist psychology is a fast-growing field, and a number of very different, sometimes conflicting approaches have developed. Such diversity is helpful. Psychology itself is diverse. It deals with a range of objects, from neurological functioning, through cognitive structure, to group attitudes and behaviour. It uses a number of different methods, including laboratory experiments, participant observation, case studies, questionnaires, and projective techniques. It operates in widely differing environments: universities, hospitals, workplaces, schools, prisons, and homes. Feminism too has many different interests, from economic and political structures through to sexuality. Feminist programmes start from requests for specific reforms, and build all the way up to calls for large-scale changes in every aspect of social relations. Different feminist psychological approaches are needed to cope with this double heterogeneity. But that does not mean that one feminist psychology is as good as another.

This book does not deal with every self-declared feminist psychology. Some writers whose work it considers do not call themselves feminists. Some do not work specifically on psychological issues. And often, one text or one person's work takes a number of different approaches, and is considered in several places in the book. I examine feminist initiatives in areas and in an order which psychology's definitions of itself suggest. I begin with what I call egalitarian feminist attempts to make traditional psychology more gender fair and therefore more scientific. Chapter 1 examines efforts within this egalitarian framework to challenge the most powerful subject in psychology, the psychologist, by pressing for more female psychologists. Chapter 2 looks at how egalitarian feminist psychology tries to balance out the discipline's 'object', the psychological subject, by studying more women and female-identified subject matter. Chapter 3 deals with egalitarian feminist criticisms of and alternatives to the male-identified methods which are the apparent centre of psychological discourse. Chapter 4 analyses egalitarian feminist attempts to extend mainstream psychology's male-oriented theories of the individual subject to include women. Chapter 5 shifts away from the egalitarian perspective, to look at what I call women-centred feminist psychologies, which present radical alternatives to both traditional and egalitarian feminist psychologies. Chapter 6 looks at how feminist psychologists have challenged the concept of the rational, unified subject, by using psychoanalytic theories of a language-structured unconscious subjectivity, and by deploying Foucault's concept of individual subjectivity as constructed and experienced through a set of discourses. Chapter 7 analyses how the associations which feminist psychology often makes between psychological and other, extrapsychological discourses, have the effect of intensifying contradictions within the traditional discipline which are important both for feminism and for psychology.

Psychology is a discipline whose main concern is testing hypotheses of similarity, and looking for statistically significant differences which falsify these hypotheses. This means that it is never able to prove the existence of a difference, only to suggest that a hypothesis of difference is supported. These characteristics are preserved in feminist psychologies, and in this book. Feminist psychologies differ in marked, significant ways from conventional discourses of psychology, and from each other. But they display strong similarities both to each other, and to the traditional discourse. And like conventional psychology, they pursue hypothesis after hypothesis, putting themselves in a state of perpetual adaptation and change, and never presenting a complete account. And so it is possible to investigate their differences from traditional psychology and from each other, but not to deliver final judgements on them as psychology, or as feminism.

Chapter one

Counting women in

We were not thinking much about being women in psychology. We simply took it for granted that women can function well in psychology in all kinds of settings, and we showed that they could by doing our work.

(Henlé in O'Connell and Russo 1983: 229)

Women . . . had to be a little better than the average man in order to stay equal. That seemed to me to be quite all right, since I was quite sure that I *was* better than the average man. That there was a gross injustice here, I preferred to overlook.

(Rioch in O'Connell and Russo 1983: 174)

In the early 1970s, women psychologists, particularly in North America, began to oppose what they characterized as psychology 'against' women (e.g. Parlee 1975). They were inspired by the contemporary growth in western feminism. Feminist writers were protesting against women's exclusion from well-paid, high-status, and meaningful work, and from cultural and political power. They were also starting to analyse subjective experiences of gender, and were finding traditional psychological accounts of them inadequate. Feminists in psychology began to investigate these gendered subjectivities, and to challenge their discipline's gender biases. The first approach they developed was what I shall call egalitarian feminist psychology.

Egalitarian feminist psychology analyses traditional psychology's errors and omissions about gender, and hopes to correct them by bringing in more female psychologists, extending male-oriented psychological work to include women, and adjusting existing procedures and theories. By extending a kind of equal opportunities policy to the whole discipline, it tries to create a gender-neutral psychology, 'a non-sexist science, a psychology of human behaviour' (Vaughter quoted in Unger 1979: 24).

Egalitarianism is the chronological and logical starting point for feminist psychology. It is also its dominant form. Its closeness to mainstream psychology is important for a discipline as concerned about its own definition and status, and as resistant to feminist ideas, as psychology generally is. Where critical psychologies have written off conventional psychology, as with marxist and other radical psychologies in the 1960s, the mainstream discipline has been able to ignore or co-opt them. The traditionalism of egalitarian feminist psychology gains it a hearing in the conventional discipline, and allows it to make changes within the established framework. At the same time, egalitarian feminist psychology departs from mainstream psychology in important ways. It is heavily indebted to western feminism. And its feminist interests in social relations link it with disciplines like sociology and history, making it more interdisciplinary than most psychology, maintaining its hopes for change and even a complete paradigm shift in the discipline (e.g. Parlee 1979, 1981). These double allegiances, to psychology and to feminism, generate a variety of goals and strategies, which allow egalitarian feminist psychology to co-exist with other forms of feminist psychology, and to assist their development.

Some feminist psychologists criticize the egalitarian approach for providing a response, not an alternative, to traditional psychology. 'Does integration lead to cooptation and dilution of feminist goals and methods?' (Basow 1986: 6), they ask. Egalitarian feminist psychology tends to neglect gender issues that do not relate to traditional psychological interest. It often treats women as a unified group, glossing over psychological and social differences between them. And it can encourage the tokenizing and co-opting of female psychologists and their work. These problems resemble those encountered by early second-wave western feminists like Friedan and the National Organization of Women, who were often slammed for trying to improve women's position within male-oriented spheres of activity, rather than pursuing female-oriented concerns. They seemed to be making women into honorary men. In the 1980s, some egalitarian feminists have responded to political constraints by reviving this approach, and only supporting gradualist, defensive, or 'new realist' campaigns around, for instance, equal employment opportunities hiring and firing. Some have even lapsed into postfeminist inaction. Such a climate increases the likelihood that egalitarian feminist psychology will be incorporated into the traditional discipline.

Because egalitarian feminist psychology wants to adapt conventional psychology, rather than replace it, it has to begin from psychology's self-definition. Different schools of psychology describe themselves differently, but the discipline's dominant view of itself is as an objective science, capable of consistent, complete explanation, and prediction. Psychology takes subjectivity, unique individual consciousness, as its object. Other western sciences exclude difficult aspects of subjectivity from their portraits of themselves, as in classical physics. Non-scientific discourses, like law and literary studies, address subjectivity by deploying their own concepts of the subject. Psychology sets out to fill the gaps left by these approaches, and in particular, to be 'a science which explains, *vis-à-vis* physics, why it is that the mind is by nature constrained initially to mislead reason in its dealings with reality' (Canguilhem 1980: 41).

Popular understandings of subjectivity, psychology's object, suggest that it escapes rationality. This makes the impossibility of sustaining an objective, scientific programme particularly clear in psychology. The fact that psychology uses 'subjective' individuals to investigate subjectivity intensifies the problem. Psychology gets round these ambiguities by ignoring them. It develops an idea of an unproblematic, purely 'psychological' subject who is rational, unified and asocial. This is a 'partial subjectivity: that which fits in with the subject-of-science of the positivist ideology of science; also, it is a subjectivity which is consistent with the rationalising subject of capitalist economic exchange' (Henriques *et al.* 1984: 141). But psychology's concept of the subject runs into a number of difficulties. Psychology takes different, sometimes incompatible, and often implicitly social subjects as its objects. These subjects emerge from psychology's links with biological, medical, psychiatric, education and employment discourses, for example. Different psychological schools also view one phenomenon, like crowd behaviour, as a manifestation of different cognitive, social, biological, or unconscious subjects. Even within one school, methodological and theoretical subjects may not match up.

Psychology also tries to deal with the ambiguities of subjectivity by imposing methodological rigour on it. It uses experiments to measure its subjects' behavioural components, and sets up psychologists as the neutral agents of these experiments. The problems here are obvious. Psychologists exert powerful influences on experiments, making the resultant data unreliable. It is impossible to define and measure every parameter of a behaviour. Subjectivity is in any case incompletely manifested in behaviours. Psychology cannot construct complete, consistent, scientific theories of the subject by adopting such a programme.

Psychology's theoretical inadequacies often lead it to replace theory with utilitarian generalizations from its most reliable methods. This utilitarianism allows psychology to adapt to its diverse and changing academic and applied contexts. Psychological utilitarianism is implemented by psychologists. By giving their work 'an evaluative aspect and a significance in terms of expertise' (Canguilhem 1980: 48), it makes them into powerful professionals. More than other self-declared 'sciences', psychology uses this expert status of its practitioners to dismiss its theoretical uncertainties, and guarantee its objectivity. And so psychologists come to dominate the discipline. They are aware of this power. Some want to expand it by making themselves indispensable within different agencies and organizations, even if this entails the loss of a clear identity as a psychologist (e.g. Herriot 1987). Most, however, support the explicit institutionalization of their expertise, through chartering, for instance (e.g. Hartnett and Shimmen 1987). In the past, psychologists have even claimed that 'the world will be saved by the psychologists, or it won't be saved at all' (Maslow quoted in Pečjak 1985: 268). Such presumptions of omnipotence are troubling, however philanthropic their tone. And, Canguilhem asks, who chooses these megalomaniac experts, who treat subjects like insects? 'How does one recognise the men who are worthy of assigning to man-the-instrument his role and function? Who selects the selectors?' (1980: 48).

The powerful place psychologists have in psychology, and the large part they play in deciding how the discipline deals with gender, has been recognized by egalitarian feminist psychologists. Their main response has been to campaign for fairer representation of women among psychologists. This chapter examines the gender imbalances among psychologists, and analyses egalitarian attempts to rectify them.

In Joanna Russ's *The Female Man*, Janet, returning to the twentieth century from an all-female future, visits the Pentagon, and asks, 'where the dickens are all the women?' (1985: 8). Walking into a parliament of psychologists, like the governing Council of the British Psychological Society (BPS), she might have had a similar reaction. There are only seven women on the forty-six strong Council.

Women's representation decreases as you ascend psychology's professional hierarchy. In Britain, women predominate in non-examination adult education psychology classes. Among psychology students at 'A' level, degree, and postgraduate level, half, 65 per cent, and 40 per cent respectively, are women. Women do slightly, but consistently, better at degree level. But there are seven male to every one female tenured academic psychologist, and women heads of department are in single figures. Women are much better represented among occupational, educational, clinical and counselling psychologists and psychotherapists, but here too they are concentrated at the lower levels of the profession.[1]

The US situation looks more hopeful. Women took two-thirds of 1982 psychology degrees and half of 1984 psychology doctorates. The Association of Women in Psychology (AWP) has about 1000 members. Many of these are also members of the American Psychological Association's (APA's) Psychology of Women Division, the largest and one of the fastest-growing divisions, which has 2000 members, almost all female. Women make up over two-fifths of APA boards and committees and over a third of its main governing bodies. But only four of the APA's twenty-six 1986 awards for outstanding work went to women. Most women in the APA Psychology of Women Division work in low-status, 'feminine', service areas of psychology. The number of psychology Ph.Ds in these expanding areas taken by women, is increasing at a particularly fast rate. Women's Ph.D parity or dominance in academic psychology has been achieved mainly through a decline in male Ph.Ds. Women hold one-third of tenure track and one-fifth of tenured posts, and still comprise only three-tenths of the total US psychological workforce. They are more likely to be low rank and part time, are lower paid, and have higher Ph.D unemployment than men.[2]

Psychology usually assumes that psychologists can act in a neutral way. Skinner, for instance, says,

> A scientist may have an effect on behaviour in the act of observing or analysing it, and he must certainly take this effect into account. But behaviour may also be observed with a minimum of interaction between subject and scientist.
>
> (1953: 21)

But worries about psychologists' neutrality continually resurface in the discipline, in a history which includes 1960s concerns with experimenter effects; 1970s ethogeny; a 1980s preoccupation with the social representations which psychologists as well as subjects draw on; and a long list of attempts to replace living with automated experimenters, from written instructions, to computers. Many psychologists realize that Skinner's optimism is excessive, and that variables like gender affect their

11

practice in important ways. They argue for a more equal representation of women and men among psychologists. Even the Scientific Affairs Board of the BPS, criticizing an initial proposal for a Psychology of Women Section, agreed that 'to encourage women to become and remain involved in the BPS is a laudable objective in itself' (Women in Psychology 1985).

Feminists often rely on male psychologists' work to solve the psychological problems they encounter. Mostly they ignore the possible significance of these male origins. Friedan's *The Feminine Mystique* (1965), which first appeared in the US in 1963, at the beginning of the second wave of western feminism, quotes male psychologists extensively and uncritically. Figes's *Patriarchal Attitudes* (1972) begins with a review of psychological and anthropological evidence on gender, pitting predominantly male experts against each other. But sometimes feminists see women's poor representation among psychologists as a problem, and attribute psychology's inadequate handling of gender to the imbalance. Greer (1971), for example, denounces psychology's gender bias by referring to the discipline's predominantly male practitioners.

Egalitarian feminist psychologists draw on both feminist and psychological criticisms of gender imbalance among psychologists. They argue that increasing the number of women psychologists will make the discipline more scientific, and will provide strong role models for other women. This approach is not new. Many early women psychologists thought that 'quietly doing our job, not as women psychologists, but as psychologists' (Henlé 1983: 229) would prepare the way for more and more women to come into the discipline, and for psychology to become fairer as a result. The approach also has precedents among other women who were the first in their fields, and has been adopted in feminist work like that of Friedan and Greer. It has emphasized an aspect of psychology that is particularly important for the discipline's status and influence. But it has had limited success. Fifteen years after it began, women are still numerically under-represented in high-status and decision-making areas of the discipline. And counting more women in among psychologists is not changing psychology's understanding of gender as much as many feminists would like.

Why is this so? First, psychology itself has resisted the campaigns. As Rioch suggests (see p. 7 at the beginning of this chapter), women psychologists always need to be better to be equal. Often they do not achieve the institutional recognition which their practice or research merit. Many of their contributions are forgotten. Where they appear to be gaining, opposition develops, based on fears about the profession's declining prestige. Humphrey and Haward, for example, warn that 'a female-dominated [clinical psychological] profession . . . could be at risk of losing status and momentum. Comparison with other female-dominated professions in the Health Service e.g., nursing, physiotherapy . . . may help to bring home this point' (1981: 413–14). Finally, the psychological profession's hostility to marriage and family commitments works strongly against women psychologists. Puffer, a nineteenth-century female psychology graduate thinking of applying for an academic post, is told by her college president, 'the rumor . . . concerning your engagement may have . . . affected the recommendation I sent'. Later, having chosen marriage over her promising career, she writes, 'The basic inhibition still operating to suppress the power of women is the persistent vicious alternative — MARRIAGE OR CAREER — full personal life versus the way of achievement' (Furumoto and Scarsborough 1986: 41). Bronstein *et al.* (1986) find that even today, where referees refer to candidates' families, they see those of female candidates as problems they have overcome, but refer to those of male candidates as assets.

The second reason why playing the numbers game with female and male psychologists does not work is that it involves equating women with feminists. O'Connell and Russo's (1983) account of eminent female psychologists, for instance, presents these women as feminist role models. Russo ends her (1982) review of US psychology of women faculties and courses with pride that these courses are being taught mainly *by* and *for* women. But female psychologists are not all feminists. Some accept the secondary status the discipline allocates them. Puffer, for instance, suggests that the restricted family life a psychological career demands is too high a price for women to pay, and urges them, instead, to study 'borderline subjects', a 'fringe of specialist research', or do consulting, criticism, and reviewing (Furumoto and Scarsborough 1986: 41). Other female psychologists conform to Laws's description of women in academia who take on male-associated traits to mask their gender. They try 'to actualise the esteemed qualities associated with the dominant group (e.g. rationality; universalism; affective neutrality; coolness; courage)', and each 'esteems herself to the degree that she succeeds' (Laws 1975: 54). Many women psychologists become honorary men. They stay close to the male-oriented tradition, particularly at higher academic levels, and assume, like Henlé at the beginning of the chapter, that their gender need not affect their career. Some psychology produced by men is more feminist than the work of these female professionals. Pleck and Sawyer

13

(1974) and Kimmel (1988) contain good examples. And Canguilhem's analysis of the power relations of psychology, which I draw on often in the course of this book, is more valuable for feminist psychology than some narrower, more science-based accounts of the discipline written by women.

A third problem with the numbers game is tokenism. The many female psychologists who adopt traditional psychological priorities make a more equal sex balance seem good sense for psychology. But although a woman psychologist may act like one of the boys, her sex never becomes irrelevant to her work. Laws describes women in academia as Tokens, made deviant first by their sex, and then their aspirations, which do not fit with social expectations about women: 'Being born female, the Token is assimilated to primary deviant status. By aspiring to the attributes and privileges of the dominant class, she becomes a double deviant: female, to be sure, but refusing the constraints of the ascribed status' (1975: 53). Tokenism allows the number of women in psychology to increase; but women psychologists remain second-class psychologists. They stay *women*: masculinized but still female — exceptions that prove the rule.

Tokenism's ambiguity constrains all women psychologists. In 1985, the women on the BPS Council argued against the establishment of a Psychology of Women Section in the Society. The Scientific and Professional Secretary issued an account of the debate to the Section's supporters, in which he quoted the women's opposition to justify the proposal's defeat. This argument managed to suggest that female and male psychologists hold principles of scientific neutrality in common, and that the BPS recognizes female and male psychologists as equal at the highest level; but also that women psychologists are different: specially suited to judge other women. In the US this ambiguity has acquired an institutional structure. Members of the APA's Division of the Psychology of Women work within the traditional professional structure, extending existing work on women, advising the APA on gender issues like the Equal Rights Amendment, and occasionally publishing papers in mainstream APA journals. But the APA is under no obligation to adopt the Division's proposals, and much of Division members' work is published outside the mainstream, in specialist journals like *Psychology of Women Quarterly* and *Sex Roles*, or in interdisciplinary feminist publications like *Signs* and *Feminist Studies*. Many Division members also work, with others, in more explicitly feminist psychological organizations, like the Association for Women in Psychology (AWP). This Association has been instrumental in getting the APA to adopt guidelines on non-sexist language and practices, and to set up an office for Women's Programmes. But it has no formal power over the APA. The BPS seems likely to establish a body similar to the Division in its Psychology of Women Section, and an autonomous organization for women in psychology may persist alongside this.[3]

The ambiguous token status of women psychologists also limits their individual reputations. Female and male psychologists often experience what Laws calls sponsor relationships, which play an important part in getting them established. But female psychologists are much more likely than male psychologists always to be seen as some male psychologist's prize student. The persistent association of Kohlberg's professional prestige with Gilligan's work is an interesting current example. A female psychologist may even reincarnate the reputation of a male co-worker, as the heightened status of Anna Freud and Carolyn Sherif after, respectively, their father's and husband's deaths, showed.[4]

Female psychologists may themselves use their token status in a restricting way. Some interpret their presence simply as evidence of their particular merit, as Rioch did; use it to justify the absence of other women; and display an exaggerated femininity. This Queen Bee syndrome was very clear with early female psychoanalysts like Deutsch, Anna Freud, Klein, Mack Brunswick and Lampl-de-Groot, whose rivalry was intense (Roazen 1985). Weaker versions of the Queen Bee syndrome still operate among prominent North American and British female psychologists. Most of the women in the APA's Psychology of Women Division are recent Ph.Ds, not yet established. And although the proposal for a BPS women's section was opposed by the women on the BPS Council, it had strong support among less powerful female psychologists, and students.

Even women who try to work as feminists in psychology suffer from the ambiguities of tokenism. Like all feminists in traditional, male-oriented fields, they trade a career, and the opportunity to make some small changes in the discipline's treatment of gender, for the scientific and social credibility they give the discipline. They also have to accept some of the discipline's traditional priorities. From the start, this conflates their egalitarian feminism with mainstream psychology's male-identified scientificity. Maccoby and Jacklin, the authors of the standard review of sex differences psychology, acknowledge that their feminism will always be incompatible with traditional psychology. But they do not question traditional psychology's male-identified emphasis on, for example, objectivity and success: 'We are both feminists . . . and

15

although we have tried to be *objective* about the value-laden topics discussed in this book, we know we cannot have *succeeded* entirely' (1974: 12–13, my emphasis). Unger depicts herself and others working in the psychology of women, as caught up in 'facho', a feminist version of macho (Arpad 1986: 208), which in their case took the form of an obsession with productivity much like that found in the mainstream: 'like the characters in *Through The Looking Glass* we are all running (and writing) as fast as we can to keep up' (1979: vii).

Female psychologists' difficult position in the discipline is an outcome of the ambiguous concept of the investigative subject which characterizes both psychology and feminism. I have already discussed the difficulties the concept presents in psychological discourse. Feminism too is centred on an impossible subject. It is caught between a variable analysis of how a female subject, 'woman', is socially and historically constructed, and a politically necessary focus on the general, permanent characteristics of this subject. As Coward says, 'the problem is that of understanding the position of women as a sex without presuming that being a sex entails forms of natural behaviour and position' (1983: 3). Feminists are more aware of this ambiguity than psychologists are of their similarly ambiguous position. Most feminists respond by multiplying the female subject, and taking the collective category of 'women' as a pragmatic basis for their politics. This category retains an idea of a unitary, rational subject, which makes 'women' a simple multiple of 'woman' (Riley 1987). But it also sustains an idea of the feminist, not just as an individual, autonomous subject, but also as a subject defined by her relationship to others, who is differently defined in different contexts, and who has no fixed boundaries. Psychology presents a much simpler, stabler picture of the psychologist-subject. Its power as a discourse ensures that this concept of the subject has more effect on feminist psychology than does the feminist concept.[5]

Egalitarian feminists who argue for more women psychologists acknowledge the contradictions in the strategy. They realize that psychology puts up powerful barriers against female psychologists; that femaleness is not the same as feminism; and that female psychologists have a problematic token status in the discipline. But they gloss over the ambiguities in the concept of the subject which underlie these difficulties. This makes them liable finally to neglect the complications of their position, and simply to accept or reject 'tokenism', without considering all its implications. Such unconscious simplifications may be a condition for their continuing to work productively within the traditional discipline.

How, besides tokenism, do psychological and feminist concepts of the subject affect feminist efforts to correct gender imbalances among psychologists? Even when psychology recognizes gender differences between psychologists, it tends to pass over other differences. It usually sees lower-valued, female psychologists, in particular, simply in terms of their sex. Differences between them are assimilated to differences on sex-differentiated traits like masculinity or self-confidence. Alternatively, the differences are related to ungendered categories of 'race', class, age, and sexuality, which are interpreted psychologically, minimizing their discursive complexity. Feminists encounter similar problems in dealing with differences between subjects. Often they simply subdivide the category of 'women' to mark differences of sexuality, 'race', age, and class. But such analyses do not take the discursive power of historical and social relations seriously enough. They render subcategories of 'women' equivalent and independent. Rowbotham *et al.*, for instance, acknowledge the complexity and contradictions of power relations, but nevertheless allocate people to one category only: 'women, blacks, trade unionists, gays, youth and national minorities' (1979: 5). Their call to feminists to recognize the interconnectedness of all forms of oppression, and to move 'beyond the fragments' to form alliances with different struggles, passes over the autonomy of different campaigns, in favour of a universal radical subject. In the light of lesbian-feminist and black-feminist criticisms of western feminism's homophobia and racism, this seems ingenuous. Such simplifications are a focus of increasing feminist concern.

Feminist psychologists, too, have tended to ignore differences between subjects across age, 'race', class, and sexuality. Female psychologists are still overwhelmingly middle-class, apparently heterosexual, middle-aged, and white. So far, feminists have mainly proposed numerical solutions to these imbalances, treating the categories as equivalent and autonomous. But many now argue that they need to deal seriously with differences between women and the power relations that produce them, and, as Hooks says, to 'assume responsibility for eliminating all the forces that divide women' (1982: 157). (See also Henley 1985.)[6]

Women first began to work as psychologists in the mid-nineteenth century. Many came from academic families, and most were employed in prestigious women's colleges on the East Coast of the US (Furumoto and Scarsborough 1986). Contemporary psychology shows a similar class imbalance. In Britain, working-class women are badly represented on full-time university psychology courses. They are more likely to study part time, in polytechnics, and to be mature students. They often study psychology after developing some expertise in it through education, community, health, or social services work, and they usually return to or take on such work, rather than becoming professional psychologists. Class bias might be expected to be less in the US, where tertiary education is less restricted and social class is often claimed to be less important. But even there, working-class women are rare in graduate psychology, and are particularly few in the higher status institutions from which most eminent psychologists come.

Psychological professions exert a particular form of class discrimination against women. Success in them demands continuous education, employment, and, as Puffer wrote, 'long, sustained, intensive application'. This in turn presupposes class-related factors like expectations of female academic excellence, and freedom from childcare, domestic work, and 'irrelevant cares and concerns' (Puffer quoted in Furumoto and Scarsborough 1986: 41). Since class is generally defined by male socioeconomic status, it is often argued that women are more able to transcend class than men. The poor representation of working-class women as well as working-class men among psychologists suggests this is not true. Do women express their class affiliations differently from men though, through fantasy, rather than exclusively through collective political resistance? Such affiliations are likely to be ignored, because they seem unfamiliar and ineffective. But this might allow them to be retained, when other class affiliations are lost. Walkerdine, recording interviews with and observing a working-class 6-year-old girl and her family in their home, uses fantasy to explore how she identifies with the family from her working-class childhood, and is at the same time distanced from it by her middle-class academic adulthood:

> Often when interviewing the participants I felt that I 'knew what they meant'. . . . Using this 'recognition' to explore the positivity of how domestic relations are lived seems to me an important step beyond assertions that the academic should side with the oppressed. . . . Such rhetoric may represent *our* wish-fulfilling denial of power and responsibility — a way of disavowing our position instead of accounting for it.
>
> (Walkerdine 1986: 191)

Beattie's (1987) popular ethnographic studies of inner-city life also show a consciousness of the psychologist's real and fantasized relationships to class. So far, though, most female and male psychologists' accounts of their class affiliations remain unwritten.

In the 1960s and 1970s, psychologists strongly criticized the discipline's predominantly middle-class constitution.[7] Today this questioning is a marginal affair. Twentieth-century western feminists, however, are always arguing about class. Second-wave feminism in Britain has drawn strength from working-class women's campaigns, like the 1968 Ford strike, the Grunwick dispute, and the women's groups active in the 1984 miners' strike. It is continually concerned about its narrow class base, and about how women's different class interests create conflicts for feminism. But its concern has not corrected these failings. And at times it criticizes class-based politics, for its omission and marginalization of gender issues. *Beyond the Fragments* (Rowbotham *et al*. 1979) was a final articulation of 1970s British feminist discontent with left, particularly Leninist politics, which sees women's oppression as the result of their absence from the labour force, interprets men's agency in that oppression as a result of their own class position, and dismisses 'bourgeois' feminism. More recently, Campbell, in her account of Conservative women, points out experiences that women of all classes share, in particular the 'generic force' (1987: 140) of women's fears of violence. She also suggests that this fear, and women's predominantly domestic, private, work experiences, generate an affinity between women and conservatism.

These diversities and shortcomings in feminist approaches to class may explain why feminists often manage only a half-hearted critique of psychology's class interests. They tend to forget these interests when using predominantly middle-class women psychologists' arguments, for example. Feminist psychologists, too, tackle working-class women's under-representation in psychology in a half-hearted way, by calling for more of them. This approach underestimates the complexity and instability of discourses of class. At best, it might produce a few working-class women psychologists who act as double tokens of both the discipline's liberalism and its anti-sexism.

Like many other disciplines, psychology is a gerontocracy. Ascending its professional hierarchies takes a long time. Progress is governed partly by disciplinary expansion or contraction, but partly also by internal professional rhythms, like length of training, and attrition, or death at the top. Age is particularly significant for women psychologists. Higher proportions of them enter training as mature students, and they take longer than men to become professional psychologists and to achieve success. This is largely because of diversions in their career paths. The eminent female psychologists in O'Connell and Russo's (1983) study who had married, had all delayed their career development in favour of that of their husbands. The few parents in the study had had children relatively late, when they had established reputations which would bridge a career break. In a fast-moving field, such breaks can be very disruptive. Female psychologists' relationships with male sponsors also depend on age. In some of the cases O'Connell and Russo describe, gender seems irrelevant: the young psychologist saw herself simply as a disciple of the older man. But the emphasis on control rather than competition in the relationships, and the sponsors' proprietorial pride, indicates their resemblance to relationships not with sons, but with high-achieving, perpetually infantilized daughters. As female psychologists grow older, however, their age becomes more important than their sex. A famous elderly woman psychologist may be seen simply as a famous psychologist. The social de-sexing of older women may contribute to this. Older women are also more likely to have acquired the male-identified characteristics that frequently accompany women's integration into psychological professions.

Psychology does not see its age bias as a problem. For some psychologists, the time needed to become a recognized practitioner or researcher is even a sign of the discipline's status. Postwar western feminism, however, is concerned about its own under-representation of younger and older women. Feminist anthologies often include a couple of pieces by young and old women. But such women also frequently work separately from women's groups where participants' age is not specified: an indication that these apparently age-free groups do not deal adequately with their interests. Feminist efforts to increase women's participation among psychologists rarely take account of age. They tend to concentrate on policies that would help women follow the same age-related career path as men. In this area, the professionalism implicated with egalitarian feminism overwhelms even its fundamental interest in numerical equity.

There are few black or ethnic minority women or men working in western psychology. The BPS does not monitor their participation. The American Psychological Association only established a Society for the Psychological Study of Ethnic Minority Issues in 1987, twelve years after it founded the Division of the Psychology of Women. Afro-Americans and Hispanics account for 12 and 6 per cent of the US population respectively, but take only 8 and 4 per cent of psychology degrees, and 4 and 3 per cent of Ph.Ds. These fractions have increased slightly over the past decade, and are larger than in other sciences. But they have to be set against an overall decline in psychology degrees, including those taken by Afro-American and Hispanic students. Psychology has attracted many fewer Asian-American students than other sciences, and its recruitment of Native-American students is negligible.

Increasing numbers of Asian-American psychology Ph.D students are working on academic topics. Among other black and ethnic minority psychology students, the tendency to take Ph.Ds in health and services areas remains strong, and is increasing more rapidly than is true for psychology Ph.Ds in general. In academic psychology, black psychologists tend to work in administration, counselling, and 'race'-related research, areas which traditionally lack status.[8] Health and services psychology are the fastest-growing and, at higher levels, the best-paid sectors of the discipline today. They are also the fields where psychologists can have most practical effects. And so black psychologists' concentration in them has positive as well as negative implications. But given the recent decline in numbers of tenured black academics, falling Ph.Ds, retention, enrolment, and grade point averages among black students, and a decreased political commitment to their education, there are unlikely to be widespread, long-term improvements in black students', professors', and professionals' positions in psychology.[9]

Psychological work on 'race' has been criticized inside and outside the discipline for deploying and strengthening dominant racist discourses.[10] But psychology still treats 'race' differences as culturally or even biologically absolute categories, and neglects the social and historical relations in which they are embedded. At best, it views 'race' as a category which, like gender, it needs to represent more fairly. In psychology, as in other professions, a black woman serves as a double token of both gender and race balance: 'You get your token woman and your token black in one *foul* swoop. You use that "black" woman as your front to other blacks. What more do you want? You've got *your* black woman, Charlie' (Hobson 1970: 74). Because black women psychologists are defined by their 'race' as well as their gender, they tend to be channelled into work of lower status than that done by white female psychologists. The fact that more black women than white women have low socioeconomic status may contribute to this marginalization, but it does not explain it. Black and white women's relationships to class are different. Family structure and attitudes about education, for instance, are more constant among black American women (Smith and Smith 1981). And 'race' tends to have stronger effects within psychology than class. While a white working-class female psychologist may take on a new professional identity which erases her class background, a black woman psychologist of any class is always distanced from such an identity by her 'race'.

Second-wave western feminism has been dominated by racist and eurocentric assumptions. Black feminists and womanists are increasingly developing their own analyses of gender. They are also bringing white feminists to examine their extreme debt to the civil rights movement, recognize their monoculturalism, and take their attention to race issues beyond a fatalistic acknowledgement of current shortcomings.[11] But white feminists still tend to acknowledge 'race' as a matter of cultural difference. This can insulate them from considering it in more political terms. Even if they do, they tend to cordon it off from other feminist issues. *Sweet Freedom* (Coote and Campbell 1987) and *Is the Future Female?* (Segal 1987), for example, include supplementary sections on black feminism, which treat it purely as a 1980s development, and have little influence on the rest of the text. Segal describes the 'powerful and effective' voices of black feminism, and argues that 'paying more attention to the needs of Black women on a practical and descriptive level, constantly being vigilant about old assumptions that ''we'' women are white, has become an important aspect of feminism in the eighties'. But she continues with an account of the difficulties of linking theories of 'race', class, and gender, and of disagreements between black feminists, and with a vague plea for white women, who cannot share black female experience, to nevertheless 'identify with' it (1987: 61, 64, 65).

Feminist psychologists too are becoming more aware that they should be dealing with 'race' differences, not as biological or cultural categories, but as historical and social relations which affect all their work. But the community of feminist psychologists is a bad advertisement for anti-racism. Its prevailing whiteness implies that it, too, sees black women as black, not women. Feminist psychology has addressed this 'race' imbalance in an egalitarian way, campaigning for more black women psychologists, and including contributions from black women in anthologies. But where black women work in feminist psychology, their 'race' often becomes, as in psychology generally, a fixed, determining contributor to their work. Their research in areas other than the psychology of 'race' and prejudice is treated lightly, particularly if it is theoretical, unless it puts questions of 'race' aside entirely and adopts a white feminist perspective. Differences between black women psychologists are ignored, even though they may sometimes be more important than their similarities. These simplifications help explain why many black women psychologists work outside feminist psychology, in black psychology, black studies, or black feminist studies.[12]

In 1975, the American Psychological Association voted to stop discrimination against lesbian and gay psychologists (Morin 1977). In 1985, it set up the Society for the Psychological Study of Lesbian and Gay Issues. These moves have had little effect on psychology's general tendency to represent sexuality simply as heterosexuality. Overall, the number of openly gay psychologists remains low. This is especially so for lesbians, though Morin hypothesizes that, because they are women, they are less troubling to the conventional discipline, and may often be ignored.

Second-wave western feminism began by neglecting or rejecting lesbianism. Greer's early notion of sexuality, for instance, was exclusively heterosexual. She used male homosexuality to denigrate conventional ideas of femininity, characterizing both as faggothood. In the 1970s, western feminism and lesbianism developed closer connections. At that time a woman-centred politics, culture, and sexuality seemed to many to be a useful tactic, or even the only worthwhile long-term goal. The mood spread as far as non-separatist feminist campaigns around disciplines like psychology. One spin-off is that many feminist psychologists still identify themselves as lesbians; half of the members of the Association of Women in Psychology, for example, are lesbians (Basow 1986). Like feminist psychologists in general, lesbian psychologists are predominantly white and middle class. This, and lesbianism's almost complete social invisibility, mitigate the shock of lesbian sexuality, and help lesbians be accepted in feminist psychology. But as with black women psychologists, feminist psychology defines lesbian psychologists almost entirely by their difference. Lesbian feminist psychologists' research focuses mainly on sexuality. When they study other topics, their sexuality tends to be interpreted as an idiosyncrasy which does not affect their work. Differences between them are rarely taken seriously. The inadequacies of this egalitarian approach lead some lesbian psychologists to work outside the Division of the Psychology of Women and the AWP, in feminist and lesbian feminist organizations which grant sexuality more significance.[13]

Discourses of 'race', sexuality, age, or class, may in some circumstances be more important influences on psychologists' work than discourses of gender. Feminist psychologists tend not to deal with these other discourses, except by adopting numerical strategies. Sometimes this restricted approach seems to emerge from a conscious limitation of political interests. Unger, for instance, suggests that 'it would be trivial psychology to politicise all interpersonal transactions' (1979: 477). Such politicizations might take feminist psychologists so far from the conventional discipline that they would lose their influence within it. Feminist psychologists' awareness of the complex discursive determinants of subjectivity is nevertheless greater than that of traditional psychologists. Unger herself argues that we need 'to look at the surroundings and systemic connections of a behavior before attempting to explain it' (1979: 478).

Feminist psychology's greater awareness of the discipline's complexities makes it more conscious of psychologists' social construction than traditional psychologists are, and more uncertain about psychologists' status as rational, unified subjects. And so it starts to uncover the difficulties about psychologists which conventional psychology tries to ignore. Psychology's theoretical uncertainties are expressed, not just in the difficulty of getting objective knowledge of subjectivity, but also in the precarious power of the psychologist who is pursuing this knowledge:

> For psychology, . . . the question of its essence, or (more modestly) of its concept, also puts in question the very existence of the psychologist to the extent that, being unable to declare exactly what he is, he finds it extremely difficult to answer for what he does.
>
> (Canguilhem 1980: 37)

This makes the distinction between powerful psychologists and relatively powerless 'subjects', the objects of the discipline, hard to maintain. Every psychologist is an object of psychological discourse, as well as an agent of it. Conversely, the diffusion of psychological knowledge makes every potential subject a psychologist too. People even act as their own psychologists, splitting themselves into professional and client-subjects to do this. Feminist psychology's consciousness of these ambiguities encourages its interest in women's representation, not just among psychologists, but among psychological subjects.

Chapter two

A balanced subject

Psychology has nothing to say about what women are really like, what they need and what they want, essentially because psychology does not know.

(Weisstein 1973: 394)

I am troubled by the rush of young researchers attempting to prove that females are not inferior to males in such-and-such an ability or such-and-such a trait, especially when it is by no means clear what difference it makes.

(Sherif 1977: 199)

Like other sciences, psychology defines itself by its object.[1] In this case, the object is the individual subject. If egalitarian feminists are fully to count women into psychology, they must address women's representation among these objects of the discipline, as well as among psychologists. But subjectivity's ambiguities produce problems with this initiative, too. This chapter explores conventional psychology's neglect of women and female-identified subject matter, egalitarian efforts to remedy these oversights, and the difficulties they run into.

Psychology studies the individual subject by isolating one variable at a time, measuring how it varies across different conditions, and controlling all other variables. The gender of a subject is treated as irrelevant, unless it is under specific investigation. But psychology always finds objectivity difficult to achieve, and gender's ubiquitous and subtle influences are particularly hard to control. And since the discipline cannot exclude psychological subjects from its accounts as it can psychologists, it has to consider the effects of gender variations among subjects more than it does among psychologists. Psychology recognizes the importance of representing women and men equally in samples, and declares itself committed to achieving a better understanding of how sex and gender affect subjects. But it does not always achieve these aims. Brown *et al.* summarize its gender-biased assumptions as follows:

1. Findings on one particular group are generalisable to individuals of other groups; therefore, the findings on males are indicative of people in general.
2. Those who are different from males are inferior to them; therefore, males are more worthy of scientific investigation than females.

(Brown *et al.* 1985: 29–30)

Psychology often neglects women. A lot of psychological theories were developed initially from studies of wholly male samples: theories of achievement motivation, moral development, and social categorization, for instance (McClelland *et al.* 1953, Kohlberg 1966, Tajfel 1979). The situation has improved over the past decade. But women are still under- or unrepresented among subjects in many areas of psychological research. Sex differences themselves are frequently seen as a nuisance, rather than a potentially interesting topic. If tests for sex differences yield no significant results, as is usually the case, they are often not reported, and are rarely followed up (Maccoby and Jacklin 1974, Borrill and Reid 1986). Established differences, however, are remembered with disproportionate force. They become explanations in themselves of female and male psychology. And they increase with citational distance from the original review (Parlee 1975, Grady 1981). Maccoby and Jacklin, authors of the standard review of psychological sex differences, note that even a study like their own, which finds mostly similarities, turns inexorably into a trait psychology (1974: 3ff), centred on masculinity and femininity, and the differences between them. The psychology of sex differences also tends to treat female subjects as inferior versions of male subjects. It uses them to test theories in high-status, male-identified areas of psychology, like achievement and self-esteem. This makes differences between female subjects seem unimportant. Like male subjects, female subjects are predominantly white, heterosexual, middle-class and well-educated, but in their case these imbalances are even more likely to be overlooked.

Psychology has a secondary tradition of studying exclusively female samples, particularly in the female-identified areas of heterosexual and parental relationships, and social and emotional attitudes and behaviours. These areas remain secondary to male-identified topics. Members of the American Psychological Association rate the work of the Psychology of Women Division as unimportant and uninteresting (Harari and Peters 1987). Women are also often portrayed as irrational, over-emotional, deviant versions of psychology's proper object, the rational, unified subject. They are 'inconsistent, emotionally unstable, lacking in a strong conscience or superego, weaker' (Weisstein 1973: 418). Psychology sometimes values female-identified characteristics positively. But here it reveals a concept of women very close to that found in dominant discourses of femininity. It views women as defined by their biology, '"nurturant" rather than productive, "intuitive" rather than intelligent . . . if they are at all "normal", suited to the home and the family' (Weisstein 1973: 418), and basically as all the same. Feminist criticisms have galvanized psychology into making more, and more positive, studies of female subjects. But the mainstream discipline still treats women subjects cursorily, concentrating on traditionally woman-identified issues like the family, ignoring many areas of women's lives, like their experiences at work and their friendships, and underestimating the importance of differences between women. It tends, too, to use its attention to female subjects as an excuse for its continued neglect of other under-represented subject groups.

The co-existence of negative and positive views of women in mainstream psychology is connected to the discipline's general uneasiness about subjectivity. For psychology, the irrationality, affectivity and sociability which it attributes to women link them to the unscientific uncertainties of subjectivity, and put them slightly outside the discipline's proper field. All the terms for different kinds of psychology, 'clinical, psychoanalytical, social or anthropological', refer to what Canguilhem, more accurately than he intended, called 'a sole and simple object of study — man' (1980: 38). But women also signify to psychology the endless rich field of research questions which subjectivity's uncertainty generates. This dual meaning of female subjects emerges most strongly when psychology tries to explain areas of intense social concern like the family, mental health, and sexuality, where the adequacy of psychology's concept of the subject comes under particular scrutiny. Women often become the embodiment of both the interesting and the insoluble questions in these areas.

How do second-wave western feminists see subjectivity? Most acknowledge that it has a power of its own, which powerfully affects gender relations, and needs to be understood. Friedan (1965) analyses women's oppression by studying their subjective experiences of constraint as wives and mothers. Firestone sees women as suffering 'emotionally,

27

psychologically' (1971: 232) as well as economically and culturally, and points out how western women's postwar conflicts have been psychologically entrenched, through for instance myths of romance. Rowbotham (1973) argues that women's isolated, unrecognized work makes subjectivity specially important to them. She suggests that although they often manage to establish a compensatory psychological, domestic power base, this is also the arena of their greatest oppression. Because of this, women's political struggles have to be connected especially closely with struggle against their 'internalizations' (Rowbotham *et al.* 1979: 75). Many feminists are concerned also with the complexities and contradictions within gendered subjectivities. Why, for instance, do women often seem to desire their own oppression? And how do psychological and social elements interrelate in our gendered subjectivities?

Feminists often turn to psychological research on gender to answer their questions, but they find its male orientation disappointing. Rowbotham questions the common psychological assumption that work is central to identity for women (1973: 90). Citing Maccoby and Jacklin, Greer argues that the gender differences mainstream psychologists have found are insignificant. She criticizes the individualist reductionism, and the ineffectualness, of conventional psychology's attempts to solve gender inequalities by manipulating female psychology: 'Psychologists cannot change the world so they fix women. Actually they don't even manage that' (1971: 90). Feminists' relationship to psychoanalysis is different. They have made extensive criticisms of its gender biases. But in contrast to conventional psychologists' shuddering rejection of everything psychoanalytic, feminists retain an interest in and commitment to psychoanalysis as an account of the intricacies of gendered subjectivities, and their development. This special relationship is examined in more detail in Chapter 6.

At times, feminist invocations of psychology ignore or even reproduce traditional psychology's gender biases. Figes (1972) uncritically takes Kohlberg's description of the highest stage of moral judgements, derived from male samples, as a guide to women's and men's psychological liberation. Friedan psychopathologizes women's frustration with domesticity, and proposes the male-identified tactics of better education and paid work outside the home as ways for them to reach the male-associated goals of high self-esteem and strong identity. Greer, like the most chauvinist of traditional psychologists, sees women's psychology as characterized by frustration, dependency and victimhood, fear, passivity, inferiority, hatred for other women, mental disorders, and bodily pathology. She wants women to pay more attention to their achievement needs, and ends with a celebration of throwing off feminine values, and taking on some masculine ones: giving up 'guilt and shame and the tireless self-discipline of women' for 'magnanimity and generosity and courage' (1971: 330). These replications of conventional psychology's misogyny come about because feminism finds it difficult to articulate links between subjectivity and political change. In the absence of an explicit theory of the connection, a concept of an autonomous, rational, individual subject very like psychology's own often emerges, by default, as feminism's object. This concept, despite its claims to neutrality, tends to carry conventional ideas about gender and other social relations with it. Western feminism is much more aware of such difficulties than psychology is. But it tends to gloss over them when it draws on mainstream psychology.

The principal feminist challenge to psychology's predominantly male subjects and masculine subject matter is, again, an egalitarian one. Feminist psychologists try to create a sex-fair psychology, which studies both women and men, and addresses female- as well as male-identified concerns. They do this by examining the traditional psychology of sex differences, and the traditional psychology of women. They tackle sex differences psychology in four ways. First, they extend its existing range, studying female subjects in areas which have previously been researched using predominantly male samples. Kohlberg's studies of moral reasoning, for instance, initially conducted with young male subjects, are still being repeated with sex-balanced samples, with conflicting results (Walker 1984, 1986, Baumrind 1986).

Feminists also criticize past studies of sex differences, and argue against common psychological assumptions about gender which are unsupported by reliable or valid evidence. Maccoby and Jacklin's *Psychology of Sex Differences* (1974) institutes a major reconsideration of the psychological studies relevant to popular and psychological ideas of gender differences. Some of these ideas are, that girls are more 'social' and 'suggestible' than boys; that they have lower achievement motivation and self-esteem; that they are better at rote learning and repetition, and worse at higher-level cognitive tasks, involving responses inhibition and analysis; that they are more 'auditory' and less 'visual'; and that they are more affected by heredity and less by environment. Maccoby and Jacklin's (1974) and later work suggests that none of these hypotheses of differences can be supported. Women differ on a relatively small number of specific measures. They have greater verbal and lesser spatial and mathematical ability, and less self-confidence and competitiveness. They tend to attribute their successes more to luck and less to ability than men, and to be more influenceable. Some of their non-verbal behaviour is different, and they display less aggression.[2] Even these differences are age- and situation-specific, and, though statistically significant, are often very small, usually considerably smaller than within-sex differences. In some areas, like spatial abilities, they even seem to be decreasing (Caplan *et al*. 1985).

The third aspect of the egalitarian feminist address to sex differences psychology is that it is increasingly trying to take the diversity of these differences into account. It is changing the traditional, biological idea of these differences, to a more variable concept of 'sex-related' (Caplan *et al*. 1985) or gender differences, which depend on age, experience, situation, and expectations. Eagly (1978) suggests that women's greater influenceability may be affected by situation factors like sex of communicator, type of information or message, task definition, and historical period, as well as process factors, like female-male differences in verbal abilities, yielding, and concern with personal relationships and group co-operation. Berg *et al*. (1981) find that women's explanations of their success are more modest[3] when they know they will be made public, and when a liked other has failed. Tittle (1986) sees adolescent girls' increasingly negative attitudes and lowered expectations of success in maths as an outcome of experiences in and outside education, and a filter for many performance differences in adolescence. Many feminists suggest that training may reduce sex differences, for instance differences in spatial ability and aggression.[4]

Fourth, and lastly, feminist psychologists try to get a more balanced picture of what established psychological sex differences mean. Horner's (1972) study of fear of success is an early example of this. Women had been found to have similar or higher achievement motivation than men, but they showed less susceptibility to techniques designed to arouse this motivation. Exploring this contradiction, Horner found that women see achievement situations as sites of a social conflict between male-identified achievement values and female-identified social values, and consequently fear success more than men. 65 per cent of female college students continued a story which begins, 'After first term finals, Anne finds herself at the top of her medical school class', by expressing conflicts about success, anticipating its present or future negative consequences, denying the student's effort or ability, ignoring the cue, or showing other 'bizarre or inappropriate responses' (1972: 161, 162). Some described a future Anne unmarried and unhappy, for instance, or told of her helping and subsequently marrying the second-ranked, male student. Only 10 per cent of male students showed such reactions to a story about a student called John. Later work complicates the picture. Sex differences in achievement arousal and fear of success may depend on the type of stimulus provided, and may be more about expectations than self-concept. And both women and men may project their ideas about gender, rather than about themselves, onto stimuli like the story above. North American women's but not men's achievement motivation seems to be aroused more by non-competitive, affiliative stimuli, but this is not true in Brazil (Maccoby and Jacklin 1974, Gama 1985).

Gilligan's *In A Different Voice* (1982) is a recent application of Horner's strategy to another area of psychology: moral reasoning. Gilligan identifies a theme of social concern and non-violence that is found mainly in women's moral reasoning, and that has been ignored in previous descriptions of sex differences in this area. Her reformulation of the psychology of moral reasoning to include this voice has acquired wide currency in feminism and in academic and popular psychological discourses. Issues of feminist and psychological journals have featured discussions of it,[5] and it has been extensively discussed on radio and television, and in popular magazines. Gilligan was even named woman of the year by *Ms* magazine in 1984. Since her work is among the most influential in feminist psychology, it demands a more detailed description.

Gilligan began from Kohlberg's (1966) stage theory of moral development, formulated from an all-male sample's responses to a set of moral dilemmas. Kohlberg later found that girls did not achieve the final stage in his series as often as boys. This supported earlier psychoanalytic descriptions of women's amorality, and Piaget's (1950) own doubts about female morality. But Gilligan discovered that girls made more relationship-oriented statements, and seemed more concerned with caring and non-violence, than boys. These traits have no place in Kohlberg's scheme. Boys, however, made more logical, decision-oriented responses, and were more concerned with rights and justice, and these male-identified characteristics form the basis of Kohlberg's classification. Gilligan's most famous example is that of two white, middle-class, relatively non-gender-stereotyped 11-year-olds: Amy, who wanted to be a scientist, and Jake, who wanted to be an English teacher. Both discussed Kohlberg's moral dilemma of a man who cannot afford the

31

expensive medicine which may save his fatally ill wife, and who must decide whether to burgle a pharmacy to get it. Jake treated the decision as an equation, trying to balance out factors like the risk of being caught and the effectiveness of the drug. Amy, however, suggested that the matter should be talked out again with the pharmacist, and that other sources of money should be looked for. Gilligan sees this as an example of the 'differences in the female voice' (1982: 185) that are ignored or undervalued by psychology. Gilligan also researched women's self-descriptions, and their decision-making about abortion, and she finds women's 'different voice' here too. Calling for 'a more encompassing view of the lives of both of the sexes' (1982: 4), she proposes that the psychology of moral reasoning, and indeed the rest of psychology, should expand to include this different voice.

Egalitarian feminism also tries to bring women into psychology's subject matter by criticizing and developing the conventional psychology of women. The APA's Division of the Psychology of Women, and the BPS Psychology of Women Section, criticize psychology's poor record of research on women's psychology, and see the rectification of this as their major field of work. Feminist psychologists have already made important contributions to the psychology of women. For example, they have reanalysed studies of mother-child bonding and maternal deprivation; have criticized conclusions drawn from them about good mother-child relations; and have extended investigations of these relations to take into account, not just maternal exclusivity and sensitivity, but children's relationships with other adults and children, and the physical, psychological and social quality of care. Feminist psychology has also tackled previously neglected areas of female experience which are relevant to its efforts to get women a better deal in men's worlds. These include mental disorder, abortion, sexuality, media representation, and experiences in non-traditional, male-identified employment.[6]

Feminist criticism and research has helped to increase the number of women subjects in mainstream European and North American psychology, and the range of topics over which they are studied. This bigger and more diverse female presence has positive effects. It makes psychology more scientific in its own terms; it improves women's standing in the discipline; and it provides feminist psychologists and feminists in general with some interesting data. But because egalitarian feminist psychology operates within the traditional discipline, it is also liable to reproduce elements of conventional psychology's restrictive view of female subjects.

Feminist psychologists tend to see the significance of gender differences much as conventional psychologists do. They, too, rarely explore no-difference findings, and grant apparently reliable differences a disproportionate significance. Even Maccoby and Jacklin (1974) use the sex difference they are most sure of, women's lower aggression, to give credence to other, less well-established hypotheses of women's lesser competitiveness and their liking for large groups. Feminist psychology also tends to concentrate on traditional, male-oriented psychological themes. It is particularly interested in fashionable mainstream topics, like attribution theory and new technology. In applied contexts, feminist psychologists frequently train women in male-identified management skills like problem-solving and assertion. Feminist counsellors and therapists often adopt similar concerns. Feminist psychologists acknowledge that low-status, female-identified traits, like nurturance and sociability, are also important for both sexes; but they do not spend much time comparing men with women on these traits. The major exception, the psychology of parenthood, displays a tendency, not in itself feminist, to equate male-identified, play- rather than care-oriented styles of parenting, with quality parenting.

Mainstream psychology's frequent interpretations of gender differences as female deficiencies are sometimes reproduced in feminist psychology. Women's lesser aggressiveness, for instance, which could be understood as a positive characteristic, is generally associated with deficits in socially-valued traits like competitiveness and achievement motivation. Feminist psychology tries to get round women's occasional lower scores on such traits by suggesting how, with the right experience and environment, they could measure up to the male-oriented norms. Apparently balanced feminist interpretations of gender differences also often reflect conventional discourses of gender. Maccoby and Jacklin (1974: 150ff) disprove the traditional psychological assumption that women have less self-esteem than men, but follow this up by subscribing to another traditional assumption: that women and men have 'somewhat different arenas for ego involvement' (1974: 159). They see individual achievement as rewarding for men, social skills as rewarding for women. But the first of these has a much higher social value and power than the second. As Weisstein says, seeing psychological gender differences as complementary is sophism: 'It is no use to talk about women being different but equal; all of the tests I can think of have a "good" outcome and a "bad" outcome' (1973: 419).

Feminist psychologists also often display a conventional psychological

33

reliance on biological interpretations of gender differences. Maccoby and Jacklin's interest in the sex difference in aggression rests largely on their belief that this difference is likely to be biologically founded. Gilligan seems at times to be suggesting that women are naturally, rather than socially, inclined towards giving relationship-oriented moral judgements. Such assumptions make gender differences seem inevitable, and reinstate the apartheid between female and male subjects that characterizes much traditional sex differences psychology.

When feminist psychologists examine areas of specifically female experience, they manage to value them more positively than the traditional psychology of women does. But this revaluation is often superficial. Berg *et al*. (1981), for instance, revalue women's lack of egotism, which has strongly negative implications in psychology, by calling it modesty. But the positive value of this female-identified modesty remains outweighed by the disadvantages which a lack of egotism implies in psychology. The feminist psychology of women also tends to put all aspects of women's experience on the same level. Russo's (1982) review of current, mainly feminist, psychology of women courses enumerates the ignored elements of women's lives on which they concentrate: birth control, abortion, lesbianism, minority women's experience, and the effects of male power and violence. Courses tend to accommodate all these categories of biological, social, and political experience under the idealized name of 'women', and to gloss over the differences and overlaps between them. As with the earlier, mainstream, psychology of women, the contemporary feminist version focuses predominantly on women's low-status roles as mothers and motherers, the biological, social and emotional facilitators of everyone around them. Feminists are aware of this restriction, but they seem unable to escape it. In spite of the increasing diversity of their work on women's experiences with children, for instance, this work remains dominated by studies of mother-child relations and the problems they encounter. Feminist psychology also finds it difficult to deal with apparent irrationalities in women's subjectivity except by pathologizing the women, or seeing them as social victims. It rejects the aspects of female subjectivity which escape conventional psychology's boundaries, or it reclaims them; but it does not address them directly.

Feminist psychology's predominantly numerical approach to sex differences and the psychology of women, can make issues of methodology and theory seem irrelevant. Investigations like those of Horner, Maccoby and Jacklin, and, to some extent, Gilligan draw on conventional, male-oriented procedures and theories. Feminists' preservation of a traditional psychological concept of the subject also means that the power involved in discourses of gender and other social relations is subordinated to a determining psychological essence. Horner does not seem to recognize that fear of success is not just a psychological variable, but also a realistic assessment of the dangers facing successful western women (Condry and Dyer 1976). Gilligan apparently views the integration of the mainly female different voice into psychology as an ethical, rather than a feminist, issue.

A frequent correlate of feminist psychology's lack of political analysis, is a conviction that changes in the purely psychological areas of perceptions and expectations can improve gender relations. But while most young women training in computing, for example, are doing word processing (Tittle 1986), changing their expectations about gender and mathematical ability can only have limited effects on their achievement. Archer (1987) suggests adopting an approach which assumes the influence of all social categorizations, rather than simply gender, on psychological subjects. But even this shift towards a wider social perspective has its downside. Because it does not challenge the psychologized nature of the categories being used, it might produce some oversimple and premature assumptions of gender similarity.

As feminist psychology becomes more popular, and extends its spheres of investigation, it is crystallizing from its mixed medical, anthropological, sociological, literary, and feminist antecedents, into a more specifically psychological form. This growing psychologism intensifies feminist psychology's professional authority even further. In psychology, it allows it to compete on near-equal terms with a crowd of other sub-disciplines. In women's and feminist studies, professionalism can have a more dramatic impact. These areas' commitment to multidisciplinary research is difficult to apply and sustain. Psychological work like Gilligan's, which is liberal, but anchored in a coherent disciplinary tradition, is often fastened on with enthusiasm. But the psychologism this encourages may help to mute feminist debate.

A further consequence of feminist psychology's psychologism, is an inadequate address to differences between same-sex subjects. As in the conventional discipline, demographic imbalances are less among egalitarian feminist psychology's subjects than they are among its practitioners. But this suggests simply that a kind of unconscious holding operation is going on among psychology's more powerful subjects. Feminist psychology repeats traditional academic psychology's concentration on

North American middle-class white student samples, and its tendency to generalize from these samples to all subjects. If women are to be a good test of male-oriented psychological theories, as egalitarian feminist psychology hopes, they must be assumed to be a largely homogeneous population. Feminist psychologists are concerned about the scientificity of this assumption. But where they address discourses of 'race', sexuality, age, and class among subjects, they seem to find them difficult to deal with on their own terms. Instead, they see them as modifying influences on gender differences. It is important to examine the specific forms these simplifications take for different social relations.

Western psychology recognizes that class differences may have effects on its subjects. But it does not look at them systematically. It usually investigates working-class subjects by testing them against norms obtained from middle-class samples. If it examines them separately, it tends to reiterate dominant discourses of working-class social or even biological deviance, by studying working-class subjects' inadequacies at work, their problems when unemployed, and their failures in education. Gender differences are often passed over in studies of working-class subjects and, for example, mental disorder (Chesler 1974). But dominant discourses of excessive yet liberated working-class sexuality and affect (Rainwater 1972) are expressed in a gender-differentiated way in psychology, in studies of working-class male crime and leisure, and working-class women's parenting. Working-class mothers' greater tendency to lie and to tell their children to hit back, for instance, is proposed as an explanation for the strong association of childhood behaviour problems with low social class (Butler and Golding 1986).

Western postwar feminism is much more concerned than psychology with how class, as well as gender, structures subjectivity. Feminist psychologists, responding to this interest, often call for more studies of working-class women and men, and for class balance in samples. Many seem to believe that lamenting the middle-class bias of their sample is a sufficient contribution towards equality. They generally pay little attention to working-class women or to class issues. But, as Archer (1987) points out, class may affect many psychological measures, like mathematical ability and childrearing practices,[7] more strongly than gender. Other widely-accepted gender differences, in for instance aggression, competitiveness, and spatial abilities, may also be influenced importantly by class. Even when feminist psychology deals with class differences, it often reproduces conventional psychology's concentration on areas which dominant discourses of class see as important, like sexuality, and attitudes to success (Rainwater 1972, Weston and Mednick 1972), and proves unable to see working-class subjects as psychologically or socially different from each other. The convenience for psychologists of middle-class student samples, and their own middle-class professional allegiances, seem to be powerful obstacles to change.

Psychological samples are also predominantly young adults. Psychology has rarely tried to correct this bias. Where it studies young and old subjects, it commonly implies their inferior status by investigating young subjects' development towards adult thinking and feeling, and old subjects' loss of these faculties. Where it studies the specific characteristics of old and young subjects, it makes age the single focus of investigation, and frequently ignores gender differences. The exception to this is the large body of work on gender differences in childhood and adolescence. But here women are represented, as in dominant discourses of femininity, as honorary mothers, preparing for reproductive hetero-sexual womanhood and the social and emotional psychological abilities that are supposed to accompany it. The much smaller amount of work on older women represents them as in mourning for the same psychological characteristics.

For feminists, the marginality of young and old women's lives is a greater focus of concern. They are interested in the experiences of these age groups, and often conduct their own quasi-psychological studies, recording individual young and old women's accounts of their lives and feelings.[8] Some feminist psychologists too are realizing that age may have important influences on gender. Self-esteem, though not significantly different between women and men throughout childhood and early adulthood, may decrease later in women's lives, for instance. Feminists are also starting to investigate specific characteristics of younger and older female subjects, like girls' strong and prolonged cross-sex identification, and older women's childcare skills. But such work often involves using older and younger women as tests of psychological theories which were developed mainly from male samples, like theories of moral development (Gilligan 1982), adolescence (Beckett 1986), transfer into the job market (Griffin 1986), and middle age (Barnett and Baruch 1985). Alternatively, feminist psychologists, like conventional psychologists, tend to study old and young female subjects in relation to events in the reproductive age-range (Ussher 1989). They study topics like older women's experiences of the menopause (Griffen 1979) and widowhood (Barrett 1985); middle-aged single women's feelings about their state (Loewenstein *et al.* 1985); and younger women's adequacy as mothers

(Phoenix 1987). The visibility such representation gives older and younger women is valuable, but the approach is too near to mainstream psychology's male-oriented and chronological age-related view of women's psychological interest to produce much of a change. This convergence with traditional psychology is also expressed in an increasingly psychological approach. The section on middle age and ageing in Williams's (1979) first edition of her psychology of women reader contained a literary piece by Sontag on double standards in social perceptions of age, and a paper on anthropological studies of the experience of menopause in women in different cultures. Six years on, in 1985, it included no such clearly non-psychological studies.

Psychology is highly reluctant to address homosexuality. APA members rate the work of the Society for the Study of Lesbian and Gay Issues even lower in importance and interest than that of the Division of the Psychology of Women (Harari and Peters 1987). Furnell (1986) found only 165 British papers on the subject between 1965 and 1985. Studies of lesbian subjects are particularly infrequent. 18 per cent of the US studies of homosexuality reviewed by Morin (1977) investigated lesbians, and a further 10 per cent examined both lesbians and gay men. Even in psychoanalysis, where different forms of sexuality are a major interest, lesbianism is rarely a central subject of study.[9] Lesbians' low social profile may partly account for this. But the convergence in lesbians of deviant sexuality and gender also encourages psychology to pass them over.

Psychology uses homosexual samples mostly to test results found with heterosexual subjects. 82 per cent of the studies Morin analyses did this. Studies also focus principally on topics on which dominant discourses of sexuality predict that gay subjects will differ, like femininity and masculinity, and parenting abilities. Where the psychological specificity of the homosexual sample group is addressed, it too is formulated in terms close to dominant discourses of homosexual difference. Sometimes psychology associates homosexuality with transsexualism, for instance: a link which expresses common ideas of homosexuals' resemblance to the opposite sex. The explicit pathologization of homosexuality achieved by homosexual treatment studies is rare now; Furnell finds none in Britain since 1979. But 95 per cent of the studies he reviews deal with the assessment, causes, and treatment of homosexuality, and in doing so, continue indirectly to define it as a problem. Studies still often address homosexuality in conjunction with child molesting. Research on lesbians is frequently preoccupied with whether the orientation is a biological aberration. Recent work on lesbian alcoholism has had to devote itself first to disproving deviancy models of this condition (e.g. Anderson and Henderson 1985).

The most positive investigations of homosexual subjects draw on a symbolic interactionist account of the language-mediated relationship between social relations and the self, to produce an account of lesbian identity. But these approaches tend to view homosexuality as a homogeneous, all-or-nothing, and ultimately psychological condition. By contrast, Freud (1920) describes homosexuality as a matter of physical and mental sexual characteristics, and object choice, which often vary independently of each other; Foucault (1979) analyses the history of particular acts' incorporation into discourses of sexual inversion, and these discourses' complementary accounts of deviance and identity; and Radicalesbians (1973) provide an account of lesbianism as political and cultural revolution.

For feminists, the acknowledgement of lesbian experience has become a central theoretical issue. Finding conventional psychological studies too sparse and negative to be much help, they often try to construct their own accounts of lesbian identity and community. To do this, they, too, often use a symbolic interactionist approach. Feminist psychologists have taken on this feminist interest in sexuality. They extend the range of psychological issues on which psychology uses lesbians to test results obtained with heterosexual women, and the range of specific aspects of lesbian subjectivity which psychology investigates. For a group of subjects who have been so hidden, this greater visibility is valuable. But feminist psychology retains conventional psychology's resistance to making sexuality a topic of frequent or serious study. Sometimes it ignores lesbianism; sometimes it brackets it together with male homosexuality. *Sex Roles'* and *Psychology of Women Quarterly's* occasional articles and special issues on lesbianism repeat the 'just like us' parallelism of conventional psychology by dealing predominantly with areas where lesbians are commonly expected to differ from heterosexual women, like gender role, relationships, work role, and parenthood. Where egalitarian feminist psychology investigates lesbians specifically, it is still largely at the stage of researching conventional topics like their biological or social construction, role differentiation, parenting, and alcoholism. Alternatively, it pursues liberal psychological and feminist interests in lesbian identity, relationships, and community, where lesbianism is treated as a self-explanatory and homogeneous category.[10]

As conventional psychological studies of lesbians become more tolerant, and egalitarian-feminist psychological studies of these subjects become more psychological, it is increasingly difficult to distinguish between the two. This convergence is limiting. It discourages investigations of specific aspects of lesbian subjectivity. It frames lesbianism as a predominantly psychological matter, an approach which marginalizes political interpretations like those of Kitzinger (1987). This psychologism also promotes neglect of differences between lesbians. Yet lesbian subjects may be more different from each other than they are from many heterosexual women. Studies which address such complexities tend to be performed in women's studies rather than within feminist psychology.

Western psychological accounts of 'race' resemble those in other discourses, but they include some important characteristics of their own. 'Race' has a history of supplementing and replacing class as a representation of deviance in psychology. As in discourses of class, deviant subjects are expected to be less abstract and rational thinkers, and more emotional, sexual, and biologically determined. But as with deviant, female gender, the visible bodily signs of deviant 'race' are taken as all-determining influences on subjects' subjectivity, and so physicality is seen as stronger in both middle- and working-class black subjects, particularly black women, than in white working-class subjects. Black women's sexuality, in particular, is often viewed as so excessive that it breaks the sublimated bonds of the healthy nuclear family and excludes black women from the category of true women.

Many psychologists have been critical of the discipline's pathologization of racial 'others'. But black and ethnic minority subjects still have low priority in psychology. Often they are simply excluded from studies, on the grounds that 'race' variations will distort findings. Sometimes they are used to test psychological norms in areas where dominant discourses suggest that they might differ from them, like cognitive development, educational attainment, mental disorder, self-concept, and family structure. And a lot of psychological research is devoted, as it has been since the 1950s, to disproving unfounded suppositions of black subjects' inferiority in these areas. Most of this work ignores gender differences.

Psychology also studies specific characteristics of black subjects. But it often appears to view black subjects as 'victims': of prejudice, of psychiatric states like 'cannabis psychosis', and of the black family. Black women are frequently cast as the sexual and familial villains in this victimology. A benign analysis of black psychology is usually reserved for characteristics which have relatively low status within psychology: for school students' high self-esteem, for instance, rather than their achievement motivation; or for supportive family and social relationships.

Like many feminists, feminist psychologists are increasingly becoming aware of their assumptions about 'race', and are trying to balance out their skewed knowledge. Stack (1986), for example, emphasizes the need to test Gilligan's hypothesis in other populations and cultures. But often, feminist psychologists draw parallels between the status of 'women' and 'black people': a comparison that effectively leaves out black women. Brown *et al*. suggest that the contemporary psychology of women puts 'race', conflated with class, in the place sex occupies in traditional psychology, leading to the following assumptions:

> 1. Findings on one particular group are generalisable to individuals of other groups; therefore, the findings on Euro-American middle-class women are indicative of women in general; and
> 2. Euro-American middle-class women are more worthy of scientific investigation than Third World women; therefore, those who are different from Euro-American middle-class women are inferior to them.
>
> (Brown *et al*. 1985: 31)

Black women also have a specific invisibility, separate from class, within the psychology of women. Brown *et al*. find that 25 per cent of the twenty-eight psychology of women books they analyse do not mention black women. The other 75 per cent all take what Brown *et al*. call a tokenist or segregationist approach, counting black women in by allocating them some scattered mentions, or a separate chapter. *Psychology of Women Quarterly*, the journal of the Division of the Psychology of Women, which features Brown *et al*.'s own review, runs other occasional articles and has devoted one special issue to black women; this, too, often looks tokenistic. As Brown *et al*. note in their study, topics are generally 'a reiteration of perennially discussed themes: the black matriarchy, the double bind of being black and female, and the relationship of black women to the feminist movement' (1985: 35). Other common areas of interest are black women's sexuality, and, particularly relevant to white middle-class feminism, black women's higher achievement motivation, and their lesser sex-role stereotyping. Feminist psychology also often accepts psychological clichés about black women: for instance, that in low socioeconomic groups they are more powerful than black men or white women; or that they are sexually delinquent (e.g. Rainwater 1972). Even if, like Cox (1981), they represent Hispanic, Native-American, Asian-American and Afro-American women's

41

experiences, they tend to treat these categories as equivalent, and ignore differences within them, which may be more important than differences between them. And what about black women's and men's specific experiences of gender? The psychology of the African family, black women's race consciousness and their sex-role development (Brown *et al.* 1985) and black feminist therapy (Johnson 1983), have been explored largely in black psychology or black women's studies.[11] Historically- and politically-oriented approaches to black women's experiences occasionally reach feminist psychology's notice, but they have not yet changed its psychologizing approach to black subjects. Feminist psychologists' current shift towards more psychological work may increase these limitations.

Feminist psychology clearly underestimates the importance and complexity of 'race', sexuality, age, and class relations' effects on its subjects and subject matter. At best, it treats these categories independently, situating psychological subjects in one or the other, or adding up their deviancies. In *Women and Psychology* (Williams 1979), for instance, Ladner's paper 'Growing up Black', which describes the specific experiences of growing up in US cities in the 1960s, has to stand for the effects of both 'race' and class on gender. Feminist psychology also tends to ignore the variable effects of particular social relations on subjects. 'Race' may be significant in some circumstances, but unimportant in others, outweighed by local factors like a particular childhood experience which produces mental disorder, or by larger influences, like an education policy which affects achievement motivation across the population. Such diversity may make it impossible to establish common psychological ground within a category like 'working-class older lesbians'. Feminist psychologists must address the social formations within which subjectivities are expressed, but they need to do so in a more careful, socially and historically detailed way.

Counting women into psychology has to be read as both an advance for feminism, and a co-option of it. The visible changes which this pro- gramme creates have some positive effects on women's place in the discipline. But on their own, they do not constitute a feminist psychology. Feminist psychologists are aware that sex balance among subjects and subject matter is not the same as gender equality, and this compels them to address gender issues in other areas of the discipline.

Chapter three

Designs for equality

Both in psychology and in society at large, masculinity and femininity have long been conceptualised as bipolar ends of a single continuum. . . . It was necessary to develop a new type of sex-role inventory.

(Bem 1974: 155)

If the issue of bias in psychological research were as simple as turning the methods and instruments prized by psychology into the service of defeating bias, many battles would have been won long ago.

(Sherif 1977: 109)

The feminist psychological initiatives which have had the most influence inside and outside psychology have all made changes to traditional methodology. This chapter looks at some of the ways in which traditional psychological methods express conventional discourses of gender. Then it examines feminist attempts to construct gender-fair methods, and the limitations of these attempts.

A science founds itself, Canguilhem suggests, on its method: 'When it became apparent that every science more or less gives itself its given, and thereby appropriates what is called its domain, the concept of a science began to place more emphasis on method than on object' (1980: 38). Psychologists themselves present method as their discipline's defining feature: 'If psychology is a science of mental life — of the mind, of conscious experience — then it must develop and defend a special methodology' (Skinner quoted in Alladin 1988: 111–12). Psychology favours an experimental model of method, which requires it to test carefully defined hypotheses against the real world in controlled, repeatable, neutral ways. It inevitably makes compromises with this methodological ideal. But the ideal is asserted in all areas of psychological method: in observations, questionnaires, interviews, and projective

43

tests, as well as experiments; and it gives them all a claim on scientific reliability. Applied psychologists, working in less controllable circumstances than academic psychologists, use the volume and social validity of data they collect to strengthen their assertions of scientificity. Even psychoanalysis, the field most criticized by other areas of psychology for its methodological irregularities, claims scientific credibility from its set rules of data collection and interpretation, and its large body of clinical material.

The connections of psychological procedures to dominant discourses of femininity and masculinity are often difficult to recognize. The power of these discourses, or a method's glamorous novelty, may conceal such associations. Many procedures are also associated with discourses of both femininity and masculinity. But, in general, traditional psychological methods tend to exclude or devalue women and the features associated with them in discourses of femininity, and concentrate on male-identified features like activity, individuality and objectivity instead.

The ideal psychologist is an active investigator, controlling the experimental environment, making specific interventions in it, and quantifying their effects. Ideal subjects are also active, expressing their psychology in measurable behaviour. In dominant discourses of gender, activity tends to be associated with masculinity, and passivity with femininity. Psychological method reproduces these connections. Its use of active procedures tends to exclude women, for instance. Levels of aggression, a highly male-identified characteristic, are usually studied in women by using passive experimental designs, which vary factors such as story content, sex of the other person in the experiment, or order of exposure to treatment. Male aggression, on the other hand, is generally investigated by more active experiments, which vary the degree of hostile, threatening, or frustrating treatment a subject experiences. Measures of female aggression tend to be relatively passive, pencil and paper responses. Men are more likely to be assessed on active behaviours like administration of electric shocks to an experimental confederate. Research on less male-identified characteristics uses fewer active methods overall. But it too uses passive tests most frequently when it is studying female subjects. Studies of interpersonal attraction, for example, use observational methods more with female subjects, and experimental methods more with male subjects (Grady 1981). The link between the notion of passive femininity and dominant discourses of biology and the natural world encourages some psychologists to take this methodological gendering further and use quasi-biological or anthropological observational procedures to investigate women. Response categories, too, are influenced by the association of femininity with passivity. Grady (1981) cites one investigation of pregnant and non-pregnant women's sexual behaviour, which used the categories 'passive', 'responsive', 'resistant', 'aggressive', 'deviant', and 'other'. The possibility of active female sexual behaviour was not even recognized.

Psychological method's de-activation of women applies in different ways to different groups of women. Mainstream psychology often attributes an agency to working-class, gay and black women that it does not allow to men in these groups. But this agency is pathologized. Psychology declares it to be fantastic, irrational and ineffective, and analyses the women's real psychological state as passive and externally controlled. Its view of such women as fundamentally, even biologically deviant, distances them still further from effective action. This ascribed passivity means that women from subordinated social groups are particularly likely to be thought unskilled in expressing themselves actively. Instead, they are studied by observation, descriptive essays or case histories, or, even more than other women, in ways which derive from biological or anthropological research.

The second aspect of dominant discourses of gender which psychological methodology reproduces, is the association of femininity and masculinity with social and individual orientations, respectively. In order to fulfil its declared aim of formulating the rules of human individuals' behaviour and experience scientifically, psychology needs principally to study individual behaviour, unaffected by social interactions. Yet its methods tend to treat only men as individuals, and women, simply as women.

Individual-oriented psychological methods, like experiments and questionnaires, often seem to discriminate against women. Women consistently score less well than men on the US Scholastic Aptitude Test (SAT). In New York, for instance, about half as many women as men win scholarships on the basis of their school leaving scores on the SAT, and women score on average sixty-two points lower on it, even though they get higher school and college grades (*Chronicle of Higher Education* 18 March 1987). Women are also severely under-represented among high scorers on the mathematics section of the test (Hiscock 1986). It can be argued that such tests are gender biased, both in their questions, which do not draw on social, female-oriented spheres of knowledge, and in their multiple choice format, which, by demanding a single answer from a set of often mutually exclusive possibilities, does not allow for women's interactive, socially responsive way of solving problems. Women's psychology is studied particularly often with socially-oriented methods. Efforts to maximize women's achievement arousal and self-esteem, for instance, frequently involve presenting them with social rather than intellectual stimuli. Researching 'the family', usually a code for studying women, means investigating women's social interactions with children, men, and other women; and social methods like observations and interviews are used particularly often in this area.

Women in socially subordinated categories are specially likely to be discriminated against by individual-oriented methods, or to be studied socially. Working-class women, for instance, score lower than middle-class women on tests like the SAT, which presuppose middle-class educational and family experiences. When psychologists study them specifically, they tend to observe them in a social, family or work context which loses sight of their individual subjectivities. Middle-class women are more likely to be studied with individual-oriented methods. Furnell (1986) notes, too, that psychology is especially likely to give social accounts of lesbian identity, while gay male identity, which is a much more serious affair, gets more individual treatment.

Conventional psychological method's association of women and sociability recognizes a specifically female psychological orientation. This can seem feminist. But the different, social methods which psychology allocates to women are not equal. They are low in status. They ignore women's non-social abilities and experiences, and the differences between women. They also lend weight to common conceptions of the absoluteness of gender differences. But if women learn their social orientation, it may not be as universal or as unchanging as these female-associated methods suggest.

Conventional psychology's principal methodological demand is for the kind of objectivity promised by the laboratory experiment. More subjective, qualitative methods, like observations, interviews, self-reports and case histories, are seen by some psychologists as a good way to address difficult-to-test aspects of subjectivity, like affect and meaning. But psychology generally views qualitative methods' social validity as less important than their lack of reliability. The methods are restricted to illustrating, supplementing, and contextualizing results obtained from quantitative procedures, and indicating future research directions. Even the pleasure their data provide may count against them.

Psychology, like other discourses, associates subjectivity with femininity, and objectivity with masculinity. Sherif (1977) describes how the status hierarchy of US psychology is related to experimental rigour, and how women are excluded from this hierarchy. The discipline 'treat[s] women, blacks and other minorities, as well as residents of certain other countries, as more "different" than a well-behaved laboratory chimpanzee' (1977: 98). During the Second World War, when Sherif became a psychologist, women were much more numerous among psychological testers than experimenters. Today they are best represented in the large but low-prestige applied sectors. Psychology also often shuts out female subjects from objective method, and leaves them to more qualitative approaches. Women in low-status social categories are especially likely to experience this. Investigations of such women frequently take the form of qualitative accounts, in their own words or in those of the psychologist, as if the distance between them and scientific psychology is so enormous that the discipline's true methods must be abandoned for preliminary, descriptive procedures.

Humanist psychology seems to avoid traditional psychology's obsession with objectivity. It addresses an area of subjectivity that mainstream psychology ignores: not behaviour, but experience, which is less easy to measure. To investigate this, it rejects scientism, and uses qualitative, rather than quantitative procedures. This departure from the rigid procedures of experimental psychology sets up a radical challenge to the conventional discipline. But humanists, too, aim for an objective science. They too try to investigate all aspects of psychological experience. They too assume that if only their methods are pursued well enough, sense can be made of the most intense, idiosyncratic experience. Some counselling psychologists claim their own forms of methodological rigour, based on intensive and long-term studies of single subjects, which they describe, in an orthodox experimental fashion, as studies 'where $n = 1$' (Murgatroyd 1982: 452). Maslow calls his experiential self-actualization workshops 'laboratories' in self-knowledge (Maslow and Chiang 1977). Rogers even tests the results of his work by using the subject-centred but still-empirical Q sort (Nye 1982). In addition, because humanist psychological method has no uniform commitment to self-description and criticism, it depends, even more than traditional methods, on the individual psychologists practising it. The psychologists' status, and their facility in argument, help enforce their interpretations.[1] Often, too, these interpretations draw heavily on conventional discourses of gender (e.g. Maslow and Chiang

1977). Such personalized gender biases are less obvious and therefore even more difficult for feminists to deal with than those in conventional psychological method.

Conventional western psychology is becoming more methodologically open. European social psychologists, for example, are increasingly concentrating on analysing language and conversation (e.g. Reicher 1984a, Potter and Wetherell 1987). The complex, idiosyncratic procedures which result are a kind of betrayal of empiricist method. But the psychologists compensate for this by claiming other kinds of reliability for their analyses. Reicher, for instance, distinguishes between a perception, which is individual and often 'openly partisan', and an account, which consists of events described in the same way by two or more sources, and which can be tested against ' "objective" indices, such as, film and photographs' (Reicher 1984b: 190). This qualified subjectivism, a sort of new man of psychological method, again retains an attachment to the objectivity of traditional methods.

Psychology's association of qualitative methods with femininity might, again, seem to have some feminist potential. But these female-identified methods too have low status in psychology. And adopting this gender-differentiated methodology involves accepting that there are stable, homogeneous relationships between women and subjectivity, and between men and objectivity: connections that are more likely to be ideological than biological. Objectivity is, in any case, always an ambiguous aim for psychological method, because of psychology's unavoidable implication in the difficulties of subjectivity. The discipline's bullish claims for male-identified objectivity never overcome its potential for 'feminine' subjectivism. This problem emerges most clearly in psychology's relationships with computer-dependent methods, which come close to its ideal of objectivity.

Computer competency has become a touchstone of good psychological method:

> The computerised method assures a standard experimental procedure for each subject . . . it minimises interaction of the subject with the experimenter. These characteristics are responsible for a desirably high degree of situational control, and assure that possible sources of experimenter bias are minimised.
>
> (Ronis *et al.* quoted in Sherif 1977: 102).

Computers can even model psychologists and subjects. Computer-dependent methods are used mainly by men, and they are mostly directed at high-status, male-identified, individual, active cognitive processes. But such methods still require an initial interaction between machine and psychologist. They still need to start with 'subjective' descriptions of psychologists, subjects, and specific mental processes like memory and language comprehension, which are then translated into a form a computer can deal with. Although psychology recognizes the resultant uncertainties in computer-dependent methods, it tends to underestimate them. But these uncertainties maintain subjective, 'feminine' elements alongside the methods' hard objectivity. Similar ambiguities feature less obviously in other psychological procedures. Experiments, for instance, rely to a much larger extent than psychologists acknowledge on the presentation and discussion of qualitative data, and on their own pleasurable, narrative characteristics. (This aspect of psychological method is explored in more detail in Chapter 7).

Procedural gender biases are a source of serious anxiety in a science as powerfully dependent on method as psychology. In the discipline's own terms, they suggest either that psychology is a young science, which is not yet over its methodological teething problems, or, more seriously, that it is a quasi-scientific discourse, constitutionally unable to overcome these problems. Some western feminists, too, are concerned about psychological method's strong affiliations to dominant discourses of gender. Greer, for instance, notes the 'arbitrary character of the test situation' in which sex differences in mental ability are measured (1971: 100). Spender (1980) criticizes Lakoff's and other psycholinguists' studies of gender bias in language and thinking, for using traditional, male-oriented measures of 'good' language. Stanley and Wise (1983) mount a comprehensive attack on social-scientific ideologies of objectivity, and what they see as their patriarchal implications. But most feminists ignore the importance of method in psychology, or merely echo psychology's own concerns. Friedan (1965) quotes social psychological surveys on women's self-esteem, without questioning the dubious methodology of this field. Figes's *Patriarchal Attitudes* (1972) is devoted to assessing evidence on gender from psychology and other disciplines, without challenging the status of this evidence. Even Greer's criticism of psychology's lack of rigour is an implicit request for more objectivity.

Feminism's attempts to explore the subjectivities of female subjects who are ignored or silenced by western discourses have led it to develop some methodological preferences of its own. It pays most attention to interviews, descriptive accounts, biographies, and autobiographies. These procedures are generating an increasingly large part of contemporary feminist literature. They are close to psychological notions of qualitative, subjective methods. But feminists often use quantitative methods as well. This involves them in the same difficulties as those faced, or evaded, by psychologists. In her study of mainly white, middle-class London lesbians, for instance, Ettore describes a tension between objectivity, which she pursues by using questionnaires, and the 'subjective' experience of lesbian identity, which she explores in interviews (1980: 13). Feminist 'subjective' and 'objective' procedures for studying subjectivity can, like the corresponding psychological methods, rest on a concept of a unified, rational, purely psychological subject, which is inadequate for their concerns.[2] But Ettore's 'subjective' voice is not so much the sound of a private individual subjectivity, as of a subjectivity constructed by its social and historical silencing. Feminist methods frequently situate themselves socially and historically in ways which distinguish the concept of the subject they work with from the one which underpins qualitative psychological methods, and which give these methods a different significance.

In psychology, some feminists stick closely to traditional methods. Their reviews of sex differences and psychology of women research often rely on conventional methodological criteria. Weisstein, for instance, criticizes the mainstream psychology of women for constructing 'theory without evidence'. She dislikes clinical method because 'years of clinical experience is not the same thing as empirical evidence' (1973: 232, 234). And she uses data from orthodox empirical experiments to emphasize the importance of social context and the irrelevance of biology to gender psychology. Unger wants to revise psychological theory, but retain psychology's emphasis on objectivity, since 'feminist scholarship can be as objective as any other scholarship with a particular theoretical bias' (1979: ix). Greeno and Maccoby call for 'the slow, painful, and sometimes dull accumulation of . . . data to show whether the almost infinite variations in the way human beings think, feel and act are actually linked to gender' (1986: 315–16). In applied psychology, feminists rely on the professionalized reliability of a situation like a clinical interview to justify their data. Psychoanalysts influenced by feminism may try to develop methods sensitive to gender-specific experiences. But they, like other analysts, give all material obtained in the professional setting of the analytic session special credibility. Feminists even sometimes implicitly accept conventional psychology's view of work on women as methodologically infantile, a kind of perpetual pilot study, by sticking to qualitative methods. Maccoby and Jacklin (1974) criticize many gender biases in psychological method. But they seem to conclude from women's and men's different areas of ego investment that the gender-divided methodologies used to discover this should be perpetuated.

The equation between good methods and traditional empirical methods is stronger in feminist psychology which addresses subjects from less powerful social groups. Sometimes it shows up in the application of particularly conventional designs to these subjects. Alternatively, a highly female-identified procedure is adopted. Brown *et al.*'s (1985) study of psychology of women textbooks found that the token pieces on black women, for instance, were divided equally between female-identified, impressionistic or experiential pieces, and studies or reviews which were preoccupied with orthodox psychological procedures. Studies of lesbians tend either to employ traditional methods like hormone measurement (Dancey 1987) or the Q sort (Kitzinger 1986), or to study women's lives in an exploratory, unstructured way.

Methodological orthodoxy seems to be the price many feminist psychologists pay to be considered psychologists. It is often more important than theoretical conformity. Feminist psychoanalysts, for instance, challenge psychoanalysis's theory much more than they change its practice.[3] Nevertheless, many feminist psychologists are criticizing the dominance of traditional, male-oriented methods and the marginalization of 'feminine' forms. Egalitarian feminist psychologists try to make the discipline fairer, by using gender-balanced procedures with both female and male subjects, and by bringing traits associated with women as well as men into psychological design.[4] Wallston (1981) suggests combining 'communal' methods like participant observation, interviews, and reports of personal experience, which are female-identified, passive, social, emotional, and qualitative, with 'agentic' methods like experiments and questionnaires, which are male-identified, active, and individual. Such an approach's insistence on dealing with non-traditional, non-objective methods points up the ambiguities which characterize psychological methods, in a persistent and useful way. It also lets feminist psychologists have and eat their methodological cake. The qualitative methods provide them with feminist validity, while the quantitative methods ensure the reliability which psychology values.

Feminist psychology's combinatory approach has been applied to experimental design as well. Sandra Bem's (1974) Sex Role Inventory, the BSRI, is an important example of this kind of initiative. Instead of using a single bipolar scale of masculinity and femininity, as psychologists did before, the BSRI asks subjects to rate themselves on three subscales, which contain either items commonly associated with masculinity or femininity, or gender-neutral items. And so the inventory can measure androgyny, high scoring on feminine and masculine subscales, and undifferentiation, low scoring on both subscales, as well as femininity and masculinity. Although women score significantly higher on femininity and lower on masculinity than men, there is a lot of overlap between female and male response distributions. And large numbers of both women and men are androgynous (29 and 21 per cent respectively), and undifferentiated (20 and 27 per cent respectively) (Bem 1977). This lack of gender specificity in sex-role self-rating, and women's and men's similar scores, suggests that it is important to measure femininity and masculinity self-ratings in both sexes.

Androgyny has been a frequent subject of western feminist speculation (e.g. Woolf 1979, Heilbrun 1982). Postwar feminism even has some methodological programmes for it, in for instance Firestone's (1971) call for a combination of aesthetic and technological modes. But feminist psychology's formalization of measurement procedures, through the BSRI and similar tests, intensified feminist interest. The ability to quantify androgyny on the BSRI seemed to some 1970s North American feminists to suggest and even to facilitate an escape from oppressive aspects of dominant discourses of femininity and masculinity, like guilt and dependency, and violence and insensitivity, which would at the same time retain femininity's positive social, emotional characteristics, and the valuable self-confidence and achievement motivation commonly associated with masculinity. Bem herself suggested that BSRI androgyny indicated 'a more human standard of psychological health' (1974: 162), transcending dominant gender schemas (1979a, b). Androgyny was expected to go along with a broad, flexible and effective repertoire of behaviours, and well-adjusted emotions. Initial studies supported this positive view, especially in the area of flexible response (Kaplan and Sedney 1980). Hypotheses of positive relationships between androgyny and emotional adjustment, achievement motivation, self-esteem and interpersonal relations, became popular starting points for research. The interest spread to other disciplines, even to such apparently distant research areas as the relationship between ratings of female singers' androgyny, and their music genre and record sleeve images (Thaxton and Jaret 1985).

Method-oriented reforms like Bem's have until recently been the feminist psychological initiatives with the broadest influence in both psychology and feminism. Gilligan's (1982) extension of psychological subject matter and theory has shown that these are not the only kinds of feminist psychology which can have an important impact. But the effect of Gilligan's work also depends substantially on its methodological innovations. Gilligan combines a traditional method of measuring moral reasoning, through standardized dilemmas, with interviews. She aims to measure relationship-oriented responses, along with the logical responses which are conventionally assessed, in both female and male subjects' moral reasoning. Her procedures draw on dominant ideas of both femininity and masculinity, in a way which puts the egalitarianism of the androgyny paradigm on a more abstract level. They are straight-forward enough examples of scientific reform to convince many psychologists, and their scientificity also bestows some vicarious rigour on feminist uses of Gilligan's work outside psychology.

Feminist extensions of conventional psychological methodology often resemble more explicitly oppositional programmes for social scientific method. Wallston's (1981) proposal is an application of Bakan's humanist suggestions for sociological method, to psychology. Gilligan, too, declares her work an attempt to expand the humanist project in psychology. Wilkinson (1986b) draws attention to the similarities between feminist and ethogenic psychological projects. Such continuities can be useful. Feminist psychologists are anxious to connect with other critical psychologies, and methodology offers an especially important means of building bridges within the discipline.

Feminist methodological innovations can have a merely cosmetic effect, however. The problem is that egalitarian feminist method, like the conventional method, centres on a concept of the subject as a purely psychological entity. This concept encourages feminist psychologists to assume that, if female- and male-identified methods and designs are applied to subjects in a balanced way, they can deal with all the gender issues in psychology. But psychology's methodological gender biases are embedded in a much wider set of gender relations, which feminist psychologists tend to underestimate.

Simply combining methods associated with femininity and masculinity, does not challenge the discourses of gender which support these associa-tions. For example, using Wallston's battery of research methods does not alter their gender associations. Locksley and Colten (1979) criticize the BSRI for claiming to change gender stereotypes, when it simply conflates them. They argue that women and men are able to rate themselves highly on cross-gender items because they continue to give them meanings consistent with their own gender roles. Bem herself has abandoned the BSRI because of its crude approach to ideas about

53

gender. Gilligan's work encounters similar problems. It suggests measuring female-identified as well as male-identified responses. But it does not directly question these identities. It echoes traditional psychology's definition of social, female-appropriate and intellectual, male-appropriate methods.

These oversimple approaches to the gendering of methods also allow the greater power of male-identified methods to be ignored. Results from male-identified methods are taken more seriously by psychologists, by the institutions that support psychological research, and by the public to whom the results diffuse. A combinatory method loses some of the prestigious closeness to scientific rigour which a feminist psychology with a conventional method retains. If, following Wallston, an attitude study includes an interview as well as a questionnaire, the interview will not achieve equal importance. Although Gilligan tries to combine humanist and experimental methods, her most quoted examples, Amy and Jake, come from a conventional experimental study of the psychology of moral reasoning, rather than from the self-concept or abortion decision interview research.

The greater power of discourses of masculinity affects psychological design, too. Feminist psychologists working on androgyny have criticized themselves for ignoring the special significance of male-identified items in the BSRI (e.g. Bem 1979a, b). Some suggest that the value of BSRI androgyny to women is simply the value of masculinity. Masculine items have higher social status than feminine items, and the BSRI masculinity scale shows the biggest correlations with other psychologically positive traits. But women's self-esteem self-ratings, unlike men's, correlate significantly with their BSRI femininity as well (Bem 1977, Heilbrun 1984). And androgyny's generally poor correlations with the traits and behaviours which were expected to relate to it, are, in general, higher with women. It seems that androgyny is psychologically and socially valuable for women (Jones et al. 1978, Kaplan and Sedney 1980), but an optional extra, and sometimes even a disadvantage, for men.[5] But, as dominant patterns of gender relations would predict, women's androgyny, or masculinity, has its limits. Women who score high on BSRI androgyny, and who show androgynous or 'blended' behaviour in sex-typed situations, are the most influenced by traditional gender schemas. Androgynous women who do not blend their behaviour are less affected by traditional ideas of gender. Men blend their behaviour less than women, but their androgyny and blending do not affect their susceptibility to traditional gender schemas (Heilbrun 1984).

Bem (1979a) suggests that paying more attention to the patterns of scoring on BSRI femininity and masculinity subscales might produce a more detailed understanding of the power which particular sex-associated traits have for women and men. In particular, it would be interesting to investigate what masculinity's significance for women rests on. But so far, the feminist psychology of androgyny has only dealt with the power of discourses of gender in its self-criticisms, not in its investigations, where it continues to address femininity and masculinity on equal terms.

Feminist psychology's methods often echo traditional psychology's broader male-oriented methodological principles. Bem and Gilligan both hope their methodological revisions will make the discipline more scientifically valid.[6] They seem to agree with Grady that 'Many issues of sex bias can be addressed by making research in psychology more scientific. . . . To the extent that the ideal of objectivity is realised, research tends to be "sex fair" in many fundamental ways' (1981: 634). Their attempts to provide more objective methods do not challenge the gender bias involved in psychological notions of objectivity. Feminist co-options of 'alternative' humanist or ethogenic methods rarely question the implicit concern with scientificity which survives in these methods, either. Feminism's frequently uncritical emphasis on empathy and understanding may even intensify the tendency of such methods to depend implicitly on the psychologist, and to be influenced by dominant discourses of gender without recognizing them.

The centring of feminist method on a unitary psychological subject makes it unable to deal adequately with differences between same-sex subjects. Usually, it ignores them. Feminists assume, for instance, that observational and interview methods mean the same to all women. But the way a method works depends on social differences apart from gender. A middle-class female psychologist, studying working-class women, affects these women differently from the way she would a middle-class female sample, where the investigation would be less powerfully connected with social surveillance and intervention. These effects are not erased by using female-identified participant observation, as well as male-identified ratings scales. A feminist psychologist's interview with and administering of a questionnaire to a young woman have stronger demand characteristics than they would have with a woman her own age. Female-identified procedures may even strengthen such demand characteristics, since they are more likely to involve the intense demands of a social encounter.

Feminist design innovations, too, have socially- and historically-specific effects. Bem and Locksley and Colten agree that sex-role inventories express ideas of gender in a particular community at a particular time, and so display built-in constraints and obsolescence (Bell and Schaffer 1984). But most psychologists working on androgyny assume that high scoring on culturally-specific scales of femininity and masculinity has a universally favourable significance, and some even use it as a yardstick of cultural development (Kaplan and Sedney 1980). In other areas, too, feminist psychologists often find it acceptable to study culturally or socially different groups by modifying item contents, but deploying the same design.

Where feminist psychologists recognize social differences, they, like conventional psychologists, tend to treat them as psychological variables of the usual sort, controllable, and equivalent to each other. They also utilize low-valued, passive, social, and subjective methods disproportionately to study subjects of low social status. 'Subjective' methods provide a politically important voice for women from socially disempowered groups, such as ethnic minority women.[7] But in feminist psychology, as in the mainstream discipline, their lack of procedural structure can reinforce existing patterns of social relations. Feminist psychologists' concentration on interviews or autobiographical writings of, for instance, lesbian women, or even the insertion of extracts from such work into quantitative studies, arrogates an interpretative power to these methodological forms which is less easy to define and challenge than the power of objective method.

Method has a central, defining place in psychology. And so it is important for feminists to address the concepts of gender which inform it. But method is not the whole of psychology, and no psychological method is intrinsically feminist or anti-feminist. The combinatory, egalitarian approach which feminist psychologists favour, often repeats traditional psychological method's own procedural macho. Many feminist psychologists are aware of a need to go beyond such simple initiatives. Feminists researching the psychology of androgyny, which is characterized by its new methodological approach to gender, have been unusually sensitive to the problems their field of study presents. Critics of Gilligan's work have recapitulated many of their arguments, indicating that an understanding of the limitations of egalitarian methodological reform is growing among feminist psychologists. Even Grady qualifies her optimism about a sex-fair scientific method by noting that 'a feminist perspective suggests a much broader awareness of the ways in which a sexist culture influences the research process' (1981: 634). Some feminist psychologists are extending this broader awareness by criticizing the 'underlying metaphysical framework' (Unger 1983: 26) of conventional method. This brings them to explore the theoretical level of psychological discourse.

Chapter four

Theory for all

Research being carried out with an eye to the development of new theory . . . is not in conflict with basic conceptual frameworks or methodological allegiances in the field as a whole.

(Parlee 1979: 127)

Psychologists of women and gender have seldom brought broader feminist theory into their work. . . . We can hope that with further growth and changes in the field will come both a more rigorous testing of new concepts and a greater interdisciplinary theoretical sophistication.

(Henley 1985: 119)

Psychology tries to produce a scientific theory of the human subject. Such a theory should give a consistent and complete explanation of the object it studies. But no theory can fulfil this ideal. Every theory has to start by drawing on other theories, in order to construct an idea of what its object is. Canguilhem describes how this theoretical dependence affects psychology:

psychology cannot, for purposes of self-definition, prejudge that which it is required to judge. Unless it does so, however, it is inevitable that, in presenting itself as a general theory of conduct, psychology will come to embody a certain idea of man.

(Canguilhem 1980: 39)

Psychology's definition of its object, the human subject, as rational and autonomous, owes a lot to other sciences' concepts of their objects. As in these sciences, the concept is always shadowed by what it excludes: a fragmentary, irrational object, which maintains a ubiquitous, unsettling, but secondary presence. Psychology also draws at times on specific ideas about the human subject which have been developed in philosophical, sociological, and, especially, biological theory.

Philosophy and natural sciences often acknowledge their theoretical influences and paradoxes. Psychology's most frequent response to its own is neglect, and a compensatory concern with rigorous, reliable methods. Often it claims that results obtained by such methods do not need formalization; that they explain themselves; and that they generate the new questions that the discipline needs. Where psychology does produce theories, they are highly specific to particular debates. Only their ambiguous, pirated concept of the individual subject links them. Psychology rarely explores these theoretical difficulties and dependencies.

Psychology is anxious to make itself more scientific by removing gender biases from its theory. But its lack of interest in theory makes it prone to overlook biases in this area. Psychological theories support two main forms of gender bias. First, their primary concept of the human subject is, itself, gendered. Wine (1985) notes the frequency with which psychological models of the subject highlight male-associated individualism, rationalism, goal pursuit, and egocentrism. Psychology's secondary subject is disunited, illogical, and female-identified. It is either ignored, pathologized, or, as in human psychology, transposed into a unified, understandable subject not far from the traditional concept.

Psychological theories' second area of gender bias rests on the associations psychology makes between the consistency and completeness of good theory, and discourses of masculinity. The proper field of women psychologists is often assumed to be far from the heights of psychological theory. Hanfmann describes 'a rather arrogant colleague' who 'told me that he knew I wrote good case histories, but had not expected me to be so good at theory' (1983: 147). Female subjects too are likely, as Gilligan says, to be left out of psychology at the theory-building stage. In 1985, the British Psychological Society expressed the opposition it saw between women and good theory, when it claimed, as partial grounds for its refusal of a Psychology of Women Section, that the psychology of women 'lacks the necessary [theoretical and methodological] coherence to be the basis of a scientific Section of the Society' (Newman 1985: 2), and questioned whether this subdiscipline had the range which a full Section of the Society requires. The Development Psychology Section lacks theoretical coherence, and it could be argued that the History and Philosophy of Psychology Section is restricted to a narrower area than the psychology of women. But theoretical criteria are interpreted particularly strictly when women are involved.

Feminism, like psychology, is structured around a defined object, gender relations. In this sense its theories, too, are scientific. As in psychology, the theories' address to their object is ambiguous. They have to understand and provide for change in gendered subjects, without assuming anything absolute about the nature of the subjects' gendering. Western second-wave feminism sometimes evades this theoretical problem, by relying on very simple explanatory frameworks, or by developing strategies for changing gender relations without bothering about theory. But many feminists argue that the full, detailed understanding which theory provides, is a prerequisite for wide-ranging change in gender relations. Feminism is less concerned with a particular model of science than is psychology, so its theory-building is less limited. Its attempts to deal theoretically with the intricacies of psychological issues have been especially imaginative. These attempts have drawn very little on mainstream psychological theory, but they have made extensive and creative use of psychoanalysis. Both characteristics have inhibited their own effects on psychology.

Feminist psychology recognizes the importance of theory more than most other psychology, and it is growing increasingly sophisticated in its theoretical approach. But it is still dominated by the attitude Parlee advises at the beginning of the chapter. It aims to reform psychological theory, until it is more gender balanced.[1] Does this strategy go far enough? Can a balanced theory exist? Does psychology need a separate gynocentric theory? And how can the irrationality of subjectivity, and its complex relationship to discourses of gender and other social relations, be addressed by a feminist psychological theory that does not question psychology's conventional, unitary, purely psychological concept of its subject? This chapter examines different egalitarian feminist attempts to deal with psychological theory's gender biases. Discourses of gender are expressed differently within different psychological theories, and feminists have responded in significantly different ways to them. I am going to begin with biologically-based theories, since these act as an implicit reference point for most psychological theories of gender.

Canguilhem describes psychology as a discipline formulated in response to physics, but modelled on biology. Biological explanations are very powerful within psychology.[2] This seems partly to be because 'human nature', interpreted biologically, is a popular last resort explanation of human behaviour. Biological factors also appear more quantifiable and stable, and therefore more scientific, than psychological or social factors. Descriptions of the anatomy and physiology of individual bodies provide a constant, unitary basis for the psychological concept of the human subject, and make it less necessary for psychologists to think about problematic social influences on this subject.

Often, as in the case of family relations and sexuality, the topics which psychology studies are gender-linked. The complicated and fast-changing nature of gender relations renders biology a particularly valuable stabilizing influence for psychological theories of this area. Biological explanations present the physical specificities of women and men as the foundation of stable and inevitable psychological differences between them. Even such apparently social differences as women's larger attendance at church and enthusiasm for coffee mornings, and men's greater participation in Rotarian meetings, are roped in to back up the argument (Hutt 1972). Women's subjectivity has a subordinate role in those accounts. Although women are a primary focus of many psychological investigations of the family, for instance, they tend to be relegated to second place in biological explanations of the results. The explanations focus on the generically male child, and reduce 'his' mother to the facilitator of 'his' psychological development. This marginalization of women seems to draw on both dominant discourses' elevation of men, as the bearers of culture, over women, the repositories of biology; and biological discourses' own low valuations of women and femininity.[3]

Biological versions of psychological theory also display more specific gender biases. Often, they employ dominant discourses of human gender to interpret other primates' behaviour, and then use these interpretations to claim continuities with human behaviour. Such interpretations pass over differences in primary social organization and ecology, and ignore the effects of particular environments like zoos and experimental laboratories. The use of Harlow's studies of caged rhesus monkeys separated from their mothers, in debates about human 'maternal deprivation', is an important example (Walkerdine and Lucey 1989). Psychology's socially-coded 'biological' interpretations extend beyond evolutionary relationships to, for instance, generalizations from the effects of sex hormones on rat behaviour, to their effects on humans. Sociobiological models of the evolutionary advantages of psychological sex differences provide still more tenuous examples. These models suggest that women's and men's subjectivities stem from female and male animals' universally different interests, in protecting their genetic investments and spreading their genes widely, respectively. The pair bond is the conflict-ridden compromise between these. The account draws strongly on dominant ideas about gender. Dawkins's description of female 'coy' and 'fast' genes, and male 'faithful' and 'philanderer' genes, is a clear example (1978: 162).[4] Sociobiology's gender biases emerge more generally in its selectivity about genetics. It does not deal fully with the counter-examples which male parenting presents to its theory; or with the fact that women, like men, have a large excess of genetic materials, and might do best by searching out new partners for each child. In addition, it focuses on the presence or absence of single genes, while the genetic control even of simple physical features is of a more complex order to this. Reproductive behaviour may also have more freedom from genetic control and be more accessible to social influence among humans than sociobiology acknowledges.[5]

Biopsychological theories tend to assimilate differences between men, and, even more pronouncedly, between women, to biology. The subjectivities of working-class heterosexual white subjects, white gay subjects, and all black subjects, are often seen as genetically-determined deviations from those of white heterosexuals. Youth and old age are viewed biologically too, as states of development and decline. Work on parenthood, like Bowlby's early studies, frequently contains an equation of women's psychological normality with biological motherhood. It specifies this biological normality further, by linking it explicitly with marriage, lack of employment outside the home, and being in your twenties or thirties; and implicitly with being heterosexual, middle class, and white. Some biological theories are sufficiently affected by increasing demands for social relevance to tackle social differences. Dawkins (1978, 1986), for instance, hypothesizes units of cultural information, memes, which undergo a quasi-evolutionary transmission through imitation. But within this framework he continues to generalize about gender, seeing all 'sexual relations as a battle' (1982: 60), an important part of the 'arms race' all genes conduct with each other.

In spite of their apparent self-sufficiency, biological varieties of psychological theory are imbued with the uncertainties which accompany any 'scientific' theory of subjectivity. The concept of the body, on which these theories centre, is also associated with female-identified excesses of subjectivity which science cannot understand. Lorenz, whose popular observational studies of animal behaviour have had extensive influence on human ethnological studies, displays a more general form of this ambiguity, when he connects nature itself, and the beauty and pleasure he finds in it, with femininity. Where he finds beauty and pleasure in male animals, he asserts their masculinity very vehemently, or else denies it. He emphasizes the aggressiveness of the male nightingale's singing, for instance, but describes Indonesian warriors' beautiful dancing as 'almost effeminate' (1978: 25). His approach to Mother Nature herself is mystical:

> it appeared to me little short of a miracle that a hard, matter-of-fact scientist should have been able to establish a real friendship with wild, freeliving animals, and the realisation of this fact made me feel . . . as though man's expulsion from the Garden of Eden had thereby lost some of its bitterness.

> (Lorenz 1978: 8)

Such combinations of a religious and a scientific approach to biology are particularly obvious in impressionistic work of this kind. But they feature in more formal studies, too.

The main challenge to psychology's biological theories comes from social explanations. These explanations try to isolate clearly-defined elements of behaviour, and to account for them in terms of the simplest possible models of learning. But they also aim to address the full range of social influences on behaviour, and this can complicate them. Social explanations constitute a second major theoretical tradition in psychology, particularly in its more social and applied areas. They oppose the conservatism of biological accounts, suggesting that, given a different environment, subjectivity might develop differently. Even strongly biologically-oriented explanations recognize that a 'multiplicity of social and cultural influences' (Hutt 1972: 133) affect psychological sex differences. But very few psychologists take a purely social approach. Most claim to be interactionists, enlisting both biological and social theories.

Unlike biological theories, socialization accounts apply equally to women and men. They do not seem to be adequate to all the convolutions of gendered subjectivities, however. Many factors which socialization theories predict will affect sex roles, like the same-sex parent's masculinity and femininity scores, parental expectations about a child's masculinity and femininity, warmth of relationship between parents and child, presence of same-sex parent, and, for boys, father absence, have contradictory or insignificant effects. Parental differences in ethnicity, class and sexuality have much less marked influences than might be expected (e.g. Pleck 1975). Some aspects of gender identity also take longer to acquire than socialization theory predicts. A full cognitive understanding of the constancy of gender across time, space and circumstances is not reached until 8 or 9 years (Kohlberg 1966), but gender reassignment is usually only possible in the first two or three years (Money and Ehrhardt 1972). To cope with these complications, socialization theories break down gender psychology into ever simpler units, and build up more and more elaborate models of learning around them. This means that variables which are difficult to measure, like media exposure and peer attitudes, and learning processes which are hard to model, like unconscious identifications, get neglected.

Socialization theories' preoccupation with creating scientific theories suggests that they are trying to beat or at least match biological theories on their own terms. Often, too, they seem to see social influences as qualifying and controlling a biologically given potential. This underlying biologism allows them to preserve traditional concepts of gender. Behaviour modification, for instance, offers the opportunity of leaving out-of-control, implicitly female-identified states behind, for the male-identified pleasures of behaviour control. Women's behavioural motivation is in addition conventionally gender-coded; they are supposed to be rewarded by attention to their physical attractiveness. And so behaviourist weight loss programmes offer both women and men the possibility of replacing the feminine body which excess weight represents, with a more masculine, in-control one, which will also provide women with some female-specific gains (e.g. Rachlin 1980).

Theories of socialization also tend to provide implicitly biological explanations of social relations other than gender. They see 'race' stereotypes as socially constructed, and suggest that whites' low expectations produce poor performance in black subjects. But they do not examine the institutional reasons for low black attainment, or study 'race' as a social category, and so they often fall into a biologically founded account of absolute 'race' differences. Although they may explain homosexuality in terms of learning, they assume a common biological basis and process for this learning, and see the condition itself as homogeneous.

Socialization theories offer the possibility of shaping and changing behaviour, including your own. But such psychological control can work as a substitute for understanding the complexity of behavioural determinants, and for other, social or political, forms of control. Since women have, in general, less social control than men, this psychologization affects them particularly strongly. Behaviourist approaches to women's agoraphobia, for instance, often concentrate on getting them to look after their family, and to work, rather than tackling the personal and social reasons for their anxiety.

The polarity between biological and social explanations of subject-ivity has been as controversial among western feminists as among psychologists. Some feminists see biology as the principal field of struggle. Firestone suggests that women's liberation requires them to become as liberated from their bodies as men are: 'Feminism is the in-evitable female response to the development of a technology capable of freeing women from the tyranny of their sexual-reproductive roles' (1971: 35). Greer too sees some aspects of female biology, like menstruation, as so negative that she wants to abolish them. Feminists who take a more woman-centred approach have developed a positive view of women's biology, and have based a full theory of gender relations on it (see Chapter 5). But egalitarian feminists tend to play down the value of biological explanations. Figes, for instance, says that 'there is almost no evidence in favour of nature' (1972: 9). The possibilities for learning and change which emerge from socialization theories fit better with egalitarian feminist commitments to balance and justice, and put these theories at the centre of many western feminist accounts of subjectivity.

Feminist socialization theories explain even the most apparently natural aspects of women's and men's subjectivity as learned. They claim that this learning operates throughout life, and emphasize how early it starts: 'the little girl is praised and encouraged to exploit her cuteness. She is not directly taught how to do it, she simply learns by experience' (Greer 1971: 75). They propose alternative lifestyles, 'the diffusion of the childbearing and childrearing role to the society as a whole, men as well as women' (Firestone 1971: 233), as ways to produce differently gendered subjectivities. Feminists tend to rely on simplistic and indivi-dualistic models of associative, reinforcement and imitation learning, which they lift from psychology and apply, unmodified, in their own work. But some develop a more intricate picture, incorporating psycho-analytic mechanisms like projection, introjection and identification, and trying to see individual socialization in a broader frame. Rowbotham, for instance, describes the contradictoriness of socialization:

> My own sense of myself as a person directly conflicted with the kind of girl who was sung about in pop songs. . . . I knew how to drop into the stereotypes we learn as female sexuality. . . . I could see through (men's) eyes but I could feel with her body. I was a man-woman.
>
> (Rowbotham 1973: 13, 41)

As in psychology, feminism's socially-oriented theories are often underpinned with a fundamentally biological idea of the gendered subject, which limits the possibilities of change. Firestone's view of gender relations as determined by reproduction is the clearest case. Greer too, in her hopes for another, truer identity for women, assumes a founding subject, based perhaps on the 'body' from which *The Female Eunuch* itself begins. Even in Rowbotham's account, conflicting ideas about identity are contained within an individual subject who decides rationally what roles to adopt in particular contexts, and historically determined learning processes operate on an original, ultimately biological, subject.

Western feminists' growing interest in differences between women is strengthening their awareness of the need for a more complex view of socialization. Such a view would go beyond the domestic, individualized, 'race'- and class-specific sphere in which feminists have often assumed all women learn to live. Feminists are also realizing that a rejection of biology can, paradoxically, increase the influence of biological determinism. As Rowbotham says, a 'defensive denial of actual difference left the way wide open for a crude and mechanical reduction of feminine potential to the body' (1973: 11). Paying attention to biology need not involve assuming that biology makes fixed contributions to psychology (Hirst and Wooley 1982), or even that all biological discourses are the same. Some feminists argue that biology's conservatism about gender is at least partly a matter of lack of feminist will. But biological characteristics still seem generally less easy to change than social characteristics, and egalitarian feminists remain more interested in social than in biological explanations.

Feminists in psychology have always had more respect for biology than have feminists in other disciplines. Some feminist psychologists have even developed a kind of biological egalitarianism as a corrective to psychology's male-oriented biological theories. Psychoanalysts like Horney, Klein, and Chasseguet-Smirgel argue that motherhood, as well as the presence or absence of a penis, is important for psychic development. Chasseguet-Smirgel (1985) suggests that a woman's ego-ideal is constructed first by identification with the mother, and only then by a redefinition of herself as the father's wife. Many academic feminist psychologists emphasize women's and men's common biological natures, and want the understanding of this to spread to men, instead of being concentrated in women, as at present (e.g. Bardwick 1972, Baumrind 1982). Some, like traditional psychologists, even claim a central place for biological motherhood in women's subjectivity: a special 'phylogenetic inheritance that makes maternity the most fulfilling role for women, at least when children are young' (Sherman 1971: 211). Generally, however, feminist psychologists try to avoid biological explanations. Weisstein declares that 'biology has always been used as a curse against women' (quoted in Halpern 1986: 1015). She dismisses hormonal explanations of sex differences because they relate poorly to behaviour, and criticizes cross-cultural studies' attempts to establish the universality of sex differences for not taking full account of cultural variety. Instead, she argues for a socialization theory which sees the individual as 'a function of what people around her expect her to be, and what the over-all situation in which she is acting implies that she is' (1973: 395). Most egalitarian feminist psychologists take a similar approach.

In feminist psychology, as in feminism and psychology generally, socialization accounts are often simplistic. Feminist psychologists are trying to correct this. Unger (1979) describes the learning of gender roles as proceeding under a complex and variable reinforcement schedule. She also emphasizes that we need to study the subtle effects which expectations about gender have on learning, particularly in the case of female-male differences whose biological nature is often taken for granted. Tittle calls for the layers of cognition which affect learning, the 'attributions, interests, values and attitudes' (1986: 1166), to be investigated. Feminists are becoming increasingly interested in how changing social influences on gender differences, through training programmes in mathematical and spatial skills, for example, might smooth out differences (e.g. Caplan *et al.* 1986, Tittle 1986). Pleck (1975) argues that the symbol-dependent aspects of socialization have been neglected, and calls for a language-oriented theory of sex-role learning. Psychologists studying social representations of gender are addressing this concern at a structurally higher level (Duveen and Lloyd 1986, Wetherell *et al.* 1987).

Some feminist psychologists are trying to understand how the illogicalities of gendered subjectivity fit into a socialization perspective. Feminist therapists analyse the complex emotional states associated with individual women's family and other social experiences (e.g. Eichenbaum and Orbach 1982, Orbach and Eichenbaum 1987). Within academic psychology, Dinnerstein's (1976) and particularly Chodorow's (1978) accounts of how gendered emotional patterns are learned have had most influence. Chodorow suggests that the concentration of childcare in women's hands brings daughters to identify symbiotically with their mothers, and to carry this interdependency and need for mutual mothering into future relationships, most especially with their own children. The emotional separation imposed between a boy and his mother is similarly transposed into his later relationships, which are marked by containment and mistrust. Chodorow hypothesizes that male involvement in childcare would change these patterns. Her view of nuclear, family-based learning makes for a neat theory, which has been highly effective in getting feminist and other psychologists to acknowledge that early emotional experiences, often neglected in their work, affect gender strongly.

More than critical accounts of class or 'race', feminism is currently an important vehicle for bringing into psychology the social questions which the discipline skates over. Feminist psychologists sometimes see it like this. Lott, for instance, says that anyone interested in making psychological theory generally more interactionist, must be interested in feminist research. Sherif (1977), Unger (1983) and Henley (1985) suggest that feminist psychology is interdisciplinary by nature, and should be much more involved with disciplines like sociology and history. But such broad understandings of social theories are infrequent. Feminist psychologists usually interpret the value of socially-oriented study in a traditional way, by assimilating it to psychology's scientific project. Lott quotes Grady: 'An awareness of the different social and economic conditions for women and men cannot be left to sociologists if psychology is to maintain its integrity as a science' (1985: 160).

Feminist socialization theories express their conventionalism most noticeably in their relationship to biology. Sometimes the theories seem to deny biology altogether. Halpern (1986) derides their apparent conviction that 'it is frightening and perhaps even unAmerican to consider the possibility that even a small part of the sex differences in spatial abilities (or any cognitive ability), may be attributed to biological factors' (1986: 1014). But as in psychology generally, most feminist psychologists see social determinants as interacting with biology. Caplan *et al.* think that the effects of training should be the main focus of research on gender differences in spatial abilities, but they connect this programme to 'a sincere wish to see what cognitive sex differences might remain if the sexes were treated without discrimination' (1986: 1017–18). Pleck notes that socialization through language requires a biological pre-adaptedness for using symbol systems. Chodorow's account implicitly sees social learning as acting on a common, biologically determined cognitive and emotional potential, through common mechanisms. It also maintains the powerful traditional link between ideas of parenting, and ideas of biological motherhood. More generally, Unger (1979), following Eagly (1978), suggests that psychological gender should always be seen as the outcome both of social or contextual, and of psychological or process factors. Unger also draws on Grady's idea of psychological 'sex' as both a stimulus variable, producing sharply different expectations of women and men, and an intrinsic subject characteristic.

Feminist psychologists' attempts to combine polarized social and biological approaches do not challenge the basis of the polarity. This remains the concept of an autonomous, rational, finally biological subject. Even feminist psychological theories which reject this biological concept completely, remain determined by it, since they define themselves by this rejection. Feminist psychological theories' inadequacies seem to be due to their close but largely unexamined relationship with this concept. It provides the theories with some parasitic scientific credibility. But it also allows the traditional power biology has within psychology to reassert itself within them. Where Maccoby and Jacklin (1974) are unable to find a social explanation for gender differences, for instance, as with female-male differences in aggression, they resort to biology, rather than leaving the issue open. It is the credibility of this biological explanation which allows them to assimilate other female-male differences to it. Even work which concentrates on the social flexibility of gender relations, often ends up making biological determinants the core of its project. Caplan *et al.*, for example, describe the pursuit of knowledge about basic cognitive differences as 'eloquent testimony to the desire for Truth' (1986: 1017).

Feminist psychosocialization theory's biologism also leads it to neglect the social and historical power relations in which gendered subjectivities are embedded. Chodorow's work, for instance, focuses on the effects of gendered family care on emotional development, at the expense of broader contexts of childcare. Bem (1983) tries to deal with such omissions with a social learning model which involves parents encouraging, in children, the construction of cognitive schemas to understand gender relations and to cope with gender discrimination, and emphasizes that this model is only a start (1984). But it is a start that plays down the complications of learning about gender and discrimination outside the family, in order to produce a viable psychological theory. Henley analyses women's and men's different patterns of touch as an expression of gender power relations, as well as of general human intimacy. She recognizes cultural and race differences in these patterns, and acknowledges the political limits of programmes to change them. But the necessity of maintaining a psychological theory leads her to reify nonverbal communication somewhat. She characterizes it as a 'micropolitical structure' in itself, which 'underlies and supports the macropolitical structure'; and she alleges that it lies at a 'crucial point' (1977: 179, 191) between open, and concealed, political control and resistance.

Feminist psychology's theoretical neglect of power relations is also demonstrated in its tendency to ignore differences in age, 'race', class and sexuality, or to deal with them in biological terms. Feminist psychologists often adopt an implicitly biological standard of heterosexual normality. Bem (1983), for example, implies that the vagina and the penis should be parallel elements in the learning of gender concepts.[6] Although Unger argues against biological explanations of homosexuality, she collapses non-heterosexual identities into a single, deviant, implicitly biological category by claiming that the 'examination of homosexuals and transsexuals and the like . . . can tell us much about how gender identity usually develops' (1979: 139). And like traditional psychology, feminist psychology tends to give socialization accounts only of homosexuality, as if heterosexuality is inborn and does not need to be learned (Morin 1977, Furnell 1986). At best, heterosexuality and homosexuality are seen as psychological variants, a perspective which homogenizes these orientations, underplays the social differences which accompany them, and takes no account of political lesbianism. Feminist psychological theories tend to gloss over class relations, too. Chodorow and Bem, for example, note their middle-class biases, but do not explore how they affect their concepts of family socialization. 'Race' differences frequently retain biological meanings in feminist psychology, under the cover of a pseudo-anthropological respect for cultural differences, or simply in default of any other meaning being articulated. It is only through feminist psychology's attention to work like Ladner's Afrocentric sociology, that it comes to consider specific features of black girls' socialization in their families and communities (Williams 1979). Some feminist psychologists analyse the negative social expectations associated with different ages, but age is also usually considered as a straightforward, strictly biological variable.

Cognitive psychological theories, which describe the purely psychological phenomena of thought structures and processes, seem to transcend the polarity between social and biological explanations. Because they provide psychology with specific, scientific theories of its own, they are in addition highly valued throughout the discipline. The growth of cognitive science, a composite discipline involving cognitive psychology and brain sciences, has raised these theories' status still further. But cognitive theories' rationalism is male-identified, drawing on dominant conceptions of the masculine nature of logical, coherent thought. This gendering is also expressed directly: because of cognitive theories' prestige, male dominance among psychologists and psychological subjects is particularly strong in them.

Although cognitive models are sometimes criticized for neglecting biology in the areas of, for instance, emotions and some mental disorders, they neglect social variables much more. Like other psychological theories, they rely on a biological concept of the subject. Even when they apply themselves to understanding the effects of social relations on individual cognition, as with work on social identity and social representations, the patterns they describe are assumed to be based on universal properties of the human mind. These patterns are usually less clear and testable than those described in overtly biological theories. Cognitive theories' defensiveness about such ambiguity makes them especially liable to stress their scientific, and particularly their biological, significance. But the biological inclinations of these theories encourage a simplistic approach to gender and other social differences. They imply that it is psychologically or biologically natural to recognize and perhaps to rank these differences. This reduces social and historical circumstances to modifying influences on a cognitive structure predisposed to differentiation and even discrimination.[7]

Feminists usually criticize cognitive science's androcentrism, and its oppressive implications for women in the areas of employment and social control, and try to correct these biases. Turkle (1984), for example, analyses how computers provide female- as well as male-identified cognitive experiences. Feminist psychologists are more insistent than most psychologists in pointing out cognitive theory's cursory approach to social factors (e.g. Sherif 1977, Williams 1985). They try to extend the theories to deal with the gender issues they gloss over. But cognitive theories' dominance within psychological discourse induces many feminists to recapitulate these theories, overlooking their subtler gender biases. Deaux (1976), for example, asserts that though the conventional, male-derived psychology of attributions should study women and women's interests more, its theories will only need extending, not reformulating. Unger, although she emphasizes that sex is a stimulus as well as a subject variable, puts both these into the service of a 'cognitive perception framework' (1983: viii). Bem (1979b, 1983) tries to impart social validity to the cognitive approach; but she still relies on a cognitive concept, that of the schema, to explain how gender relations become an integral part of subjectivity. Gilligan extends Kohlberg's cognitive

71

theory of moral reasoning, proposing a separate, mainly female stage sequence, which develops through increasingly complex social, rather than logical, concepts. As she suggests, this supplementation produces a creative tension or uncertainty in the theory. But the linear structure of her stage sequence does not present an alternative to the structure of Kohlberg's theory: it merely parallels it.

Even when gender differences require Byzantine elaborations of conventional cognitive theory to explain them, feminist psychologists tend to ignore the possibility of a specifically female cognitive structure. And what about the diverse subjectivities that each gender includes? Gilligan recognizes, but does not theorize, the cultural particularity of her work. The specificity of cognitive accounts of particular ages is so strong that feminist psychologists have not really managed to make links between them or across them. How can general theories of cognitive deterioration and social withdrawal relate to theories which stress the specificity of women's work and family experiences? How does Kohlberg's theory of gender identity development, drawn on by many feminist theorists, fit with feminist social learning and psychoanalytic models of gender identity? Feminist cognitive theories also pass over the aspects of subjectivity, particularly female subjectivity, which mainstream cognitivism declares irrational, and outside its boundaries. Finally, in feminist as in conventional psychology, cognitivism helps perpetuate an idea of gender distinctions as inevitable and biological: 'The human race can be divided rather easily into two groups of males and females. A consequence of this fact is the development of cognitive categories to describe and process gender-related information' (Deaux *et al.* quoted in Condor 1986a: 6). Such assumptions place limits on the changes in gendered subjectivities which Bem, for instance, hopes can happen at the cognitive level.

What about self-styled alternative psychological theory? The most influential current here is humanist psychological theory, which opposes traditional psychology's dedication to rationality, and its current rampant cognitivism, with a more subjective approach. It views the subject as a holistic entity, suggests that it encompasses consciousness as well as behaviour, and is interested in the interpersonal as well as the individual aspects of this consciousness. But although humanist theory takes as its object all the elements of subjectivity which empirical psychology's concept of the subject excludes, it does not thereby challenge the structure of this concept. Its relative freedom from the demands of traditional methodology even produces what is in some ways a stronger account of an autonomous, integrated subject, which includes both objective and subjective characteristics. And like conventional psychology, humanist psychology retains an idea of the subject which can be isolated from social considerations for the purposes of creating a truly scientific psychological theory. Humanist psychologists realize that gender relations affect this subject. They often sympathize with feminist critiques of traditional theory. But they assume that deep down, 'human potential' is universal, and that because they address this potential, they are themselves irreproachably feminist. Psychic potential is a socially specific concept, however, unlikely to escape the influence of discourses of gender and other social relations. Often humanist theory simply draws on popular ideas about gender and gives them a psychological reading. It claims that individual growth can take different, nurturance- or achievement-oriented forms for women or men respectively, and offers women minimal growth programmes congruent with this division. Women fully occupied with children, poor and under stress, may be advised to pursue personal growth within these limits, taking five minutes each day for themselves, to read the newspaper, drink coffee, or relax, for instance.

Western feminists are often interested in humanist psychological theories. Friedan (1965) uses Maslow's hierarchy of needs to show what women are being deprived of, and makes the self the focus of her arguments. Firestone's (1971) final chart of revolution shows, under the heading 'ultimate goal', 'happiness', then self-determination, and then 'realisation of the conceivable in the actual'. Rowbotham (1973) suggests that women's and men's psychology contains a basic humanity that, however distorted, is valuable, and needs to be freed. Rowbotham *et al.* are humanistic psychologists in their approach to consciousness. We need to bring personal issues to the surface and examine them 'out in the open', they say. This notion of psychological self-help becomes the basis for their feminist politics (1979: 136), the means whereby individuals and collectives can insert themselves into gaps in existing power structures. Rowbotham *et al.* recognize that consciousness is not a consistent, unitary entity. 'The feminist approach to consciousness perceives its growth as many-faceted and contradictory' (1979: 109). Rowbotham, too, realizes that her idea of an autonomous, dissident figure is male-identified and individualized, and that not all women or men become feminists simply by consciousness-raising. But these restrictions are not always remembered. Rowbotham *et al.* devalue the role of ideology and signification, on the grounds that they are more distant and theoretical than consciousness. This takeover of feminism by humanist psychological theories limits its ability to see subjects as socially, historically, or even psychologically different, since, ultimately, every subject has the same potential for consciousness and change.

Feminist psychology is aware of humanist theory's marginality. It is itself a marginal discourse, struggling for legitimacy. Perhaps for this reason, it rarely commits itself entirely to a humanist framework. It tends rather to co-opt aspects of humanist theory for its own ends, and to employ more traditional theories as well. Nevertheless, its programmes for reforming theory often recall humanist psychological theories. Gilligan, for instance, redefines humanist interests in subjective and interpersonal experiences, as gender-fair interests. Unger, who adopts a fundamentally social-cognitive theory, argues that sex-specific psychological mechanisms restrict everybody's 'personal growth' (1983: ix). This convergence between humanist and feminist psychological theory allows feminists to work in humanist psychology, and to make minor revisions of it. But it can stop them seeing its underlying gender biases. Humanist psychology's caution about change can add to egalitarian feminist psychology's existing theoretical timidity. A humanist feminist psychology also risks reproducing humanist theory's psychological reductionism, particularly when it tries to build a general feminist theory from humanist psychological values (e.g. Tronto 1987).

Psychology often tries to resolve theoretical difficulties by avoiding theory completely, and making utility, not truth, the measure of its success. Reliable method becomes the discipline's unifying factor, and theory turns into just another methodological tool, deployed for its effects, rather than its scientificity. This emphasis on what works is especially strong in fields which have not developed coherent theories, like the psychology of industry and advertising. Western psychology developed partly in response to the social and political need for individuals to monitor and correct their own and each other's behaviour and attitudes (Canguilhem 1980). The psychology of child development, work, and educational testing are obvious examples (Riley 1983, Hollway 1984, Rose 1985). Utilitarianism agrees well with these adaptational functions. But it is no solution to psychology's theoretical difficulties. As Canguilhem says, 'the efficacy of the psychologist . . . lacks a firm foundation as long as it cannot be proved to derive from the application of a science (1980: 37). Even more than the theories discussed before, utilitarianism ignores the problematic issue of the discourse's scientific object, the subject. In its case, this results in a picture of psychology as completely opportunistic, 'a mixture of philosophy without rigour, ethics without obligation and medicine without control' (Canguilhem 1980: 37).

Utilitarianism itself depends on some specific, unrecognized assumptions:

> It has to be recognized . . . that in order for the idea of tool to exist, there have to be ideas that are not in themselves tools, and that in order to attribute a certain value to a tool, it necessarily follows that not every value is that of a tool limited to the production of others.
>
> (Canguilhem 1980: 48)

Psychological utilitarianism's assumptions are hard to recognize, because they come so close to popular discourses of the individual, and of gender and other social relations. Its criteria of a subject's effectiveness, for instance, are generally success at prestigious work, which is commonly associated with masculinity, and success in personal relationships, particularly long-term heterosexual and parental relationships, which is associated with femininity. The male-identified criterion, the one associated with dominant social categories, or categories that 'work', is the one on which utilitarian psychology concentrates.

Feminism is always too concerned with social change to be only utilitarian. But second-wave western feminists display this approach at times. Like psychologists, they start to see theory as a tool, and to adopt male-identified criteria of its effectiveness – a frontier spirit of quest and progress, for instance:

> In order to explore, we need good maps . . . 'Abstraction' should help us to move when we wish and to settle in the best camping places. It should help us to communicate and spread experience, feelings, understandings and ideas and thus facilitate action. It should not be a series of coded sign-posts that only a small élite can decode and which lead us round and round in circles.
>
> (Rowbotham *et al*. 1979: 54, 55)

Feminist psychologists, too, sometimes adopt a utilitarian approach. Weisstein (1973) implicitly accepts this approach when she criticizes conventional psychological theories for *not* working. Some feminist therapy offers a pick-and-mix set of opportunities for women to become more effective, in work and relationships, on the board, at the sink, or wherever personal or social inclination puts them. Effectiveness in such projects is linked with male-identified achievement, and the different achievement options are themselves structured by dominant discourses of gender; but these gendered associations are passed over (e.g. Dickson 1982). A feminist utilitarianism is even less able than other forms of feminist psychology to challenge the difficult founding concept of the psychological subject. Its insight is limited by its rejection of theory. But the approach can allow feminist psychologists to produce considerable small, short-term changes, by following in the tracks of existing, effective, male-oriented theories, and modifying them slightly.

Feminist psychology is becoming conscious of its theories' unadventurousness, their distance from other feminist debates, and the way their focus on individual subjects forces them to neglect social relations. Calls for more sophisticated, dialectical, cultural, psychoanalytic, and reflexive perspectives are becoming more frequent.[8] Feminist psychologists are also increasingly concerned to avoid dogmatism and prescription. Fine, for instance, declares that there can be no universal laws for feminist psychology. She calls on us to 'document the diversity of women's experience, and not reify an essential argument about gender' (1985: 179). Unger (1983) argues that epistemological certainty is feminist psychologists' main enemy. She advises them not to stick to scientism, but to draw on dreams, fantasies, and utopian wonderlands as well. This would produce the heterogeneity which she believes feminist psychological theory needs. Without it, the theory underestimates the strength and complexity of gender's place in psychology. But feminist psychology, like traditional psychology, is still dominated by a love-affair with certainty. Feminist psychologists' confidence in their explanations is good for morale, and sometimes it is tactically necessary. And feminist psychologists are still predominantly concerned with making egalitarian corrections to traditional psychological theories, rather than working with their uncertainties.

In a discipline like psychology, which insists on the specificity of its vocabulary, procedures and concerns, feminist initiatives which stay close to the traditional discipline are valuable. They can challenge psychology intimately, in debates which matter to it. But throughout psychology, in the areas of theory, method and subject matter, and among subjects and psychologists, the egalitarian feminist approach provides striking examples of the problem of double deviance. It is not taken seriously as academic or professional psychology. And it seems to many to take feminism's unavoidable compromises with traditional discourses to unacceptable levels, and to be out of touch with feminism outside psychology. In response, feminists have developed more wide-ranging, less faithful addresses to psychology. Sometimes, interventions in a discourse may be more effective when they come from outside.

Chapter five

Woman-centred psychology

> Women, being in touch with the sense of cyclical change and the life cycle, may be well equipped to see how things need to be integrated, what factors are needed for the development of others, how things flow from one another, how we can keep in touch with our humanness.
>
> (Cutmore-Smith 1986: 33)

> It is important to study the areas in which women have been neglected or in which their treatment has been biased, but one should not make a fetish about the quasi-religious, unique properties of women.
>
> (Unger 1979: 479)

The constraints of egalitarian feminist psychology have led some feminists to develop a woman-centred approach. Rather than taking over or adapting old forms of psychology, these feminists hope to create a psychology of their own, which, by addressing specifically female aspects of subjectivity, will empower women. More and more women psychologists are adopting aspects of this programme.

Woman-centred psychology is grounded in a particular woman-centred form of western feminism. This version of feminism sees the key to changing gender relations, not in increased female access to existing power structures, but in resisting these patriarchal structures from outside, and liberating women's specific political, cultural, or biological potential. As Kaplan says, it transforms the meaning of femininity within feminism, from shameful submission, to proud resistance (1986: 11). The woman-centred perspective had some impact at the beginning of the second wave of western feminism, but it was in the 1970s that it became most powerful, and most in conflict with egalitarian approaches.[1] In the later part of the decade, its theories and campaigns seemed to many to be the only active and innovative part of the western feminist movement, and affirming or rejecting it occupied an enormous proportion of feminist writing and talk. The political limitations of the approach, in particular its inability to deal with differences between women, have made it less powerful than it used to be. However, cultural aspects of woman-centred feminism in work like that of Rich (1977), Daly (1979), Dworkin (1981), Griffin (1982) and Spender (1982), remain influential in western women's movements, particularly in the US.

Cultural woman-centred feminism attacks dominant cultures' concerns with logic and aggression, which it sees as inextricably connected with their maleness. It celebrates a 'feminine' culture of pacifism, art, empathy, and spirituality, in which all women can potentially share. Sometimes it also recognizes the specificity of different women's cultures within this female world. But it places so little emphasis on resistance to the dominant culture, that it either becomes a sort of 'toothless liberalism' (Segal 1987: 24), or ignores politics completely. This inattention to politics allows even egalitarian feminists to adopt woman-centred arguments when dealing with cultural issues. It makes woman-centred feminists' hypotheses about differences between women seem tokenistic. At times it brings woman-centred feminism into alliance with postfeminist discourses, in which gender politics are similarly softpedalled. And it strengthens woman-centred feminism's influence within other discourses which set themselves apart from political concerns, like psychology. For this reason, the chapter concentrates on cultural, rather than on political, articulations of woman-centred feminism.

Like egalitarian feminists, woman-centred feminists think that psychology is important for feminism. They argue that 'women are the only oppressed people whose biological, emotional and social life is totally bound to that of the oppressors' (Morgan 1970: xxxii). Again, like egalitarian feminists, woman-centred feminists believe that subjectivity is an important part of gender relations. But their concept of subjectivity is more woman-identified. This gynocentrism combines with their psychologization of gender to make raising female consciousness their primary interest. Morgan, for instance, introducing her collection *Sisterhood is Powerful*, says that women need to explore personal experiences, find their 'own consciousness', (1970: xxvii), theorize it, and then extend this consciousness-raising process. Female self-actualization becomes the means to feminist revolution.

Woman-centred psychology like Miller's *Towards a New Psychology of Women* (1976) tries to take both woman-centred feminism and egalitarian feminist psychology further, by creating an alternative, female-specific psychology.[2] It intensifies debate about gender differences, and acts against the pacifying, inoculating effects egalitarian feminist psychology often has. This makes it seem more feminist than egalitarian feminist psychology, and much further away from the traditional discipline. But the main effect is to make it more diverse than other forms of feminist psychology, despite the certainty of its pronouncements. The differences between it, and traditional and egalitarian feminist approaches, are not as big as they look. Woman-centred, traditional, and egalitarian feminist psychologies all define their subjects as rational and autonomous, and ultimately ground them in biology. These commonalities lead woman-centred psychology, like egalitarian feminist psychology, to maintain some connections with the mainstream discipline; to produce criticisms of traditional psychology which resemble those of egalitarian feminism; and to co-exist with egalitarian feminist psychology, much more frequently than woman-centred and egalitarian approaches co-exist within feminism as a whole.

The shared concept of the subject also leads woman-centred psychology to repeat, in a clearer form, many of the problems of egalitarian feminist psychology. Although woman-centred psychology revalues traditional psychological discourses of femininity positively, it fails more conspicuously than egalitarian feminist psychology to challenge their contents. Its concern with celebrating femininity encourages it to pass over more of traditional psychology's gender biases than egalitarian feminist psychology does. And because it assumes that gender differences are biologically or culturally fixed, it is especially likely to neglect psychological or social differences between women, to take female subjectivity as defining feminism, and to treat psychology as a form of social action in itself. Eichenbaum and Orbach, for instance (1982), suggest that feminism can start on the inside, with women's individual or group psychological consciousness, and proceed outwards to political campaigning. This chapter will explore how woman-centred psychology reformulates yet repeats different elements of traditional and egalitarian feminist psychologies, beginning from the agent of psychology, the psychologist.

Egalitarian feminist psychologists sometimes argue against the assimilation of feminists into existing psychological professions, and for their separate organization. Walsh emphasizes how this has advanced women's position in US psychology, and suggests that it still provides a needed 'anchor of outrageousness' (Albin quoted in Walsh 1985: 24).

But such an argument is reactive rather than affirmative. It implies that if circumstances were less oppressive, women could work with men. Woman-centred psychologists are more convinced of the value of separate working. They claim that female psychologists have something special to contribute by virtue of their sex, and they often see work done by women as feminist simply because women do it. They turn Miller's (1969) plea for psychologists to give psychology away, into an attempt to give psychology away to all women. They co-opt areas of psychology which rely on female subjects, like early psychoanalysis, for feminism, arguing that these women are the real scientists in these fields, the real psychologists. Alternatively, they view women psychologists as contributing to feminist psychology only when they work in a culturally woman-identified way. In the academic sphere, this might involve working in women's colleges, or, more generally, using female-identified subject matter, method, and theory. An increase in women's numerical representation is therefore given a biological or cultural, rather than an egalitarian, justification. Some woman-centred psychologists think, too, that only a woman should study female subjects, and that she should do so as much as possible, because only she can understand them. Shainess (1970) criticizes work on women's psychology done by men for serving male interests, and wants women to do more in this field.

Some aspects of the woman-centred interpretation of female psychologists' place are justified. The single-sex environment of mid-nineteenth-century US women's colleges seems to have provided a uniquely supportive environment for the first women psychologists, for example (Furumoto and Scarsborough 1986). But woman-centred psychology's commitment to bringing women into the ranks of psychologists as emblems of femininity has a number of drawbacks. From the perspective of traditional psychology, such psychologists are, even more than egalitarian feminist psychologists, reassuringly marginal. At best, they may be granted a specific validity, as experts in feminine psychology. Many woman-centred psychologists evade this difficulty, because they choose to work outside psychology, in women's studies, or outside academia, in practically-oriented women's organizations. But wherever she works, a woman-centred psychologist's sex does not guarantee her feminism, any more than it does for an egalitarian feminist psychologist. As Shainess (1970) accepts, female psychologists may collude with male-oriented psychology against their own interests. The possibility that male psychologists might collude, against *their* interests, with a female-oriented psychology, is recognized less. Most woman-centred psychologists doubt men's ability to produce a woman-centred discipline. But a woman-identified psychologist, male or female, is in any case still a psychologist, and shows traces of the male-identified authority this position carries.

Woman-centred feminists recognize that feminism's concept of the gendered subject as both a social construct, and an absolute essence, is ambiguous. But their definition of the female subject as a biological or cultural essence leads them to pursue this ambiguity much less than egalitarian feminists. Their essentialism has been the main focus of criticism from other feminists. In psychology, it is intensified by the discipline's own essentialism about the individual subject. It causes woman-centred psychology to be much more restricted to the concept of a purely psychological subject than egalitarian feminist and even some traditional psychologies are. This apolitical essentialism allows many woman-identified psychologists to work in mainstream professional and academic institutions. It lets them operate as egalitarian feminist psychologists at times, too. A psychological conference on women at work can appeal to 'women-centred decision makers and administrators', and at the same time can present an egalitarian feminist agenda, including 'feminist management theory/feminist occupational psychology', 'mobility for career couples', and 'intimacy needs of career women' (National Women at Work Conference 1987: 398).

Counting women in among feminist psychologists on the grounds of their biological or cultural femininity also neglects differences between them. This omission has strong precedents in woman-centred feminism generally, as well as in psychology. Morgan's *Sisterhood is Powerful*, for example, recognizes the need to transform feminism so that it addresses the interests of women outside its predominantly white, middle-class constituency, and includes contributions from women outside it. But it remains prone to generalizations: 'we share a common root as *women* . . . capitalism, imperialism and racism are *symptoms* of male supremacy – sexism' (1970: xxix, xxxix).

Where woman-centred feminists address class specifically, they often equate femaleness with an oppressed biological 'sex class', set up working-class women as the embodiment of this class, and finger middle-class women as sell-outs to the male sex class. Where woman-centred feminism recognizes 'race' differences, it frequently tries to describe 'race'-specific female essences, and in the process layers on clichés about, for instance, black women's victim or matriarch status, in a way which mythologizes the women and denies difference and change. The only area of difference between women which woman-centred feminists consistently address is that of sexuality. Woman-centred feminism asserts the historical and contemporary ubiquity of lesbians. Often, too, it describes lesbianism as the epitome of the woman-centred approach, as if, by carrying identification with women into the most intimate areas of experience, lesbians crystallize feminist resistance: 'A lesbian is the rage of all women condensed to the point of explosion' (Radicalesbians 1973: 471). This interest in lesbianism preserves the emphasis dominant discourses of femininity place on women's sexuality. It challenges these discourses, too, by valuing women's active sexuality positively, and by defining lesbianism very broadly, as a matter of political or cultural identity, rather than simply of sexual relations (e.g. Rich 1980). But this definition ignores the possibility that lesbianism might have different meanings; for some, it might be a matter of object choice but not of political or personal identity. The definition also collapses very different female-identified resistances together. As black, and white working-class lesbians have pointed out, it tends to reduce lesbianism to the dominant white, middle-class politics and culture of lesbianism.

Psychology's own reluctance to acknowledge social differences renders woman-centred psychology's denial of differences between women more intense than that of woman-centred feminism generally. Woman-centred psychologists think all female psychologists are women first. They are more likely than other psychologists to define themselves as lesbian. But they are just as likely to be white, middle-class, and middle-aged. Some woman-centred psychologists argue that women of different ethnic backgrounds, classes, and ages need to be represented fairly among them, in order for their work to be truly woman-centred. They are often more zealous than egalitarian feminist psychologists in pursuing this representation (e.g. Cox 1981). But as in egalitarian feminist psychology, such subcategorizing of femininity is no answer. Does belonging to a particular social category, or asserting your identity with it, really guarantee that your psychological research represents that category? Is a declaration of being a lesbian, and a dedication to researching lesbian subjects, enough to make your work intrinsically lesbian-centred? This approach assumes that female psychologists in a particular category are all the same. It ignores the different interests held by women within the categories of 'black women', 'young women', and 'lesbians', which Morgan recognized when she compiled her book. 'It was important', she says, 'to have more than one voice speak for so many sisters, and in differing ways' (1970: xxx). The approach also

83

ignores the specific discursive structures of woman-centred psychology. The lack of young women committed to a consistently woman-centred psychology, for instance, indicates not just that this psychology needs to spread its feminine community wider, but that it is a historically-specific product of late 1970s debates within western feminism, and that it, like other branches of psychology, is a profession in which experience counts.

Egalitarian feminist psychologists are increasingly following Gilligan in their 'effort to ask a different question' from 'How much are women like men? Or, how much do women deviate from a male-defined standard?' (1986: 325) (see also Baumrind 1982). Sometimes they see a focus on a specific female psychology as a necessary transitional phase (Beloff 1980), or a powerful defence against the 1980s anti-feminist resurgence (Hyde 1985). Woman-centred psychology takes this further, arguing that female subjects and femininity should comprise the entire subject matter of feminist psychology. They are helped in this by numerous addresses to women's particular subjectivity in feminism outside psychology. Greer, for example, describes women as particularly likely to transcend 'the basic alienation of man from himself' (1971: 113), and as able to think outside, as well as inside, logical categories. And she reinterprets the 'low sense of ego' psychologists describe in women, as a positive characteristic: 'What a blossoming! If women had no ego, if they had no sense of separation from the rest of the world, no repression and no regression, how nice that would be!' (1971: 111). Daly (1979) claims an elemental Self for women, and suggests that a form of spiritual bonding characterizes their interactions. Spender (1982) believes that women's thinking takes a special subjective form that cannot be formalized in men's language. Haug (1987) interprets daydreams as a specific, neglected feature of women's psychology, which have the potential to produce feminist utopias and other resistances.

Woman-centred psychology takes the biologically female subject as its sole object. But female subjects do not guarantee a wholly woman-centred approach. Studies of female samples may still reproduce traditional psychology's male-oriented interests. Orbach (1978), for instance, suggests that the solution to women's eating problems is for them to develop more positive feelings about their physical, sexual, intellectual, and social selves. This emphasis on individualism and self-esteem comes close to traditional male-oriented therapeutic programmes. Many woman-centred psychologists try to avoid such male-identified parameters. They aim to explore and celebrate, not just those elements of discourses of femininity which the traditional and egalitarian feminist psychologies of women focus on, but also those which they ignore or reject. They transform a wide range of female-identified areas of experience, like fantasy and madness, listening, silence, and inefficient or nonsense language, sexuality, reproduction and motherhood, menstruation, and social and emotional relationships, into productive essences of femininity. They are even optimistic about conflicts between women, on the grounds that paying attention to them can produce gains in feminine self-realization (e.g. Caplan 1981, Orbach and Eichenbaum 1987).

Woman-centred feminists' idealization of femininity makes their work on subjectivity inflexible and socially limited, and allows traditional ideas about gender to sneak back in. This is particularly obvious in Daly's 'Catholic . . . discourse and rhetoric' (Segal 1987: 18), which attributes purity and degeneracy to women and men, respectively. Woman-centred psychology, too, is generally happy to assume that men's 'cultural and biological experiences are mostly different from those of women' (Aitkenhead 1987: 299), and to adopt conventional ideas of what these different experiences entail. Marshall's (1984) championing of women managers' distinctive co-operative skills, for example, remains very close to conventional organizational psychology's idea of these skills, although it assesses them more positively. Woman-centred psychology is affected by the traditional psychological notion that women's femininity rests on their bodies. As a result, it is dominated by biological topics, like motherhood and menstruation. It is difficult to evade the dominant culture's stranglehold on these topics. By remaining intensely, almost pleasurably absorbed by their intractability, woman-centred psychology often helps sustain them in their present state. Its accounts of anorexia, for instance, are dominated by descriptions of how dominant discourses of femininity link a narrowly defined physical attractiveness to female sexuality and success. They try to value denigrated body images positively (Orbach 1978), and to emphasize the valuable place eating has in women's relations with others, especially other women (Chernin 1986). But in the end they maintain the conventional strong association between body and self-image. Sometimes they even set up a physical image very close to conventionally-desirable femininity as an implicit goal (Diamond 1985).

Occasionally, woman-centred psychologists recognize that their notion of an essential feminine subjectivity is problematic. Shainess, for instance, begins her consideration of gender psychology by asking, 'Who is Eve?' (1970: 257). She, like other woman-centred psychologists, does not pursue this question, but she manages to write as if she knew the answer. Woman-centred psychologists are also interested in language and the unconscious, in spite of the misogyny which they see in linguistics and psychoanalysis. These areas of study engender more complicated ideas about the subject than do other psychological fields. But woman-centred interpretations tend to link them simply with femininity. Sherfey (1970), for instance, identifies psychoanalytic repression with the suppression of female sexuality. This move does away with the productive uncertainty which the concept of the unconscious can introduce into psychology.

Woman-centred psychology is also unable to deal adequately with differences between its 'feminine' subjects. Sherfey (1970) points out that femininity may not be a transhistorical absolute; but her certainty that it exists now endows it with contemporary universality. Caplan (1981) describes mother-daughter hostility as varying greatly across cultures, and is unsure whether it is culturally universal. But she emphasizes cross-cultural similarities in women's nurturant roles. Eichenbaum and Orbach (1982) note that conventional conceptions of feminine experience are socially limited. But they relegate their consideration of 'race' and class to an appendix, and collapse the two together. As in egalitarian feminist psychology, white, middle-class, middle-aged, heterosexual women are the main subjects of woman-centred psychology. Woman-centred feminism's predominantly cultural form in psychology, allied to the discipline's traditional lack of interest in sexuality, allowed woman-centred psychology to ignore homosexuality at first; Miller (1976) equated sexuality with heterosexuality. Today, lesbians are more likely to be studied in woman-centred than in egalitarian feminist psychology. But the diffuse culturalism of the woman-centred definition of lesbianism induces woman-centred psychology to study the emotional satisfactions and positive self-image associated with lesbianism, rather than sexuality (e.g. Cox 1981, Mannion 1981).

Woman-centred feminism's interest in female-identified investigators and subjects, and psychology's centring on method, encourages woman-centred psychology to reproduce aspects of traditional methods without discussing their gender biases. Woman-centred therapy, for instance, tends, like orthodox psychotherapy, to use a regulated, male-identified structure of fixed-length sessions in which the exploration and resolution of conflicts is controlled in the last instance by the therapist. But woman-centred feminists outside psychology place strong emphasis on method. Many think, like Stanley and Wise (1983), that women should be doing feminism, rather than learning or theorizing it. They quote Lorde, 'The master's tools will never dismantle the master's house' (Moraga and Anzaldúa 1981), and suggest that women should work, not by 'adopting masculine methods which are not incompatible with the masquerade of femininity', but with 'genuine womanpower' (Greer 1971: 114, 115). They try to create alternatives to male-identified procedures, which involve taking women's personal experience as the basis for feminist speech, writing, and action, and using 'small groups, circles rather than rows, centres as information and research services, open newsletters' (Rowbotham *et al.* 1979: 75).

These experience-centred procedures echo forms of organization used in other resistances; Rowbotham (1973) notes their connections with libertarian socialism, for example. They also draw on the qualitative, communal, agentic approaches of humanist psychology, and redefine them as feminine. They are the most powerful aspect of woman-centred feminism. They allow woman-centred feminism both to recognize diversity among subjects, and to tie this diversity together in the name of shared feminine experience. Their written forms, like autobiographies, biographies, and interviews, make up a large part of contemporary western feminist literature. Their experiential forms, in particular consciousness-raising, have become closely identified with feminism itself. They have even started to feed back into humanist psychological method (Kippax *et al.* 1988).

Egalitarian feminist psychologists often revise psychological methods, but they reject the possibility that feminist psychology needs a specifically woman-centred method. Lott (1985), for example, despite her interest in the specific psychological questions posed by women's experience, rejects calls to feminize procedures. But because methods are what psychology judges itself on, a woman-centred psychology needs to address them. Many woman-centred psychologists respond to this need by developing specifically feminine procedures.

Woman-centred psychological procedures resemble those used by woman-centred feminism generally, but they draw even more on the humanist psychological tradition. Douglas, researching how sex-role attitudes affect therapy, calls on Bakan's and Reason and Rown's anti-objectivist methodological programmes. She suggests that the 'subjective, intuitive, emotional' (1986: 29) methods they defend are rejected by psychology because they are associated, not with lack of scientific rigour, but with femininity. She reclaims these methods for woman-centred psychology. She also appropriates 'the usual psychotherapeutic methods – genuineness, warmth, empathy, clarification, confrontation, to name a few' (1986: 30). Eichenbaum and Orbach (1982) draw on the case-history tradition in psychotherapy, and on woman-centred feminism's interest in individual accounts. They present short narratives of women's lives, and claim them for feminist therapy on the grounds that they emerge from women's personal experience. Woman-centred psychologists also criticize the gender bias of traditional psychological method. They get much angrier about this than egalitarian feminist psychologists do. Douglas, for instance, reviewing research on how sex-role attitudes affect therapy, says,

> The toys they were using were called analogues, adjective check-lists and pseudo-clients with fake case histories . . . the rules are such that all discovery and exploration is blocked through the control and manipulation of the 'subject' and the relevant variables to obtain relevant data.
>
> (1986: 28, 29)

And she warns that 'any involvement in boys' games can be contaminating' (*ibid.*).

To many psychologists, woman-centred methods look very unpsychological. But they provide simple correctives to the gender bias which psychology itself recognizes in its methods, and they recall a recognized minority tradition in psychological methodology. Their reduction of feminism to individual women's experiences can seem simplistic to egalitarian feminists, but their clarity and adventurousness interests them. This double appeal is turning woman-centred methods into the most persuasive and influential aspect of woman-centred psychology. But the methods present severe difficulties for a feminist psychology. Like traditional psychological methods, woman-centred methods idealize individual subjects, isolating and containing them. Personal change is equated with feminist change. This idealization of individual subjects is clearest in autobiographical accounts or case histories, but it is apparent in reports of interviews or group work, impressionistic observations, or speculative essays, too. It encourages woman-centred psychologists to ignore the wider discursive structuring of methodology, and to assume that revaluing a traditionally female-identified method positively guarantees its feminism. But such a revaluing leaves the method's conventional gendering unchallenged. When traditional psychology's negative idea of associative, 'intuitive' methods is reformulated positively, for instance, its links with dominant discourses of femininity remain unchanged.

Links with traditional psychology's male-identified scientism are sometimes preserved in woman-centred methods. Even when Douglas asserts that as a researcher she will inevitably influence her research findings, she mentions that this happens 'in sub-atomic physics' too (1986: 29). Woman-centred methods also tend to rely uncritically on the particular kinds of scientificity that therapeutic and humanist methods have developed. Douglas promises to 'use naturalistic observation of everyday clinical practice', and 'use Psychotherapeutic skills', without questioning whether the methodological standards she is invoking here might themselves be gendered. She even adopts uncritically an apolitical, humanist version of psychological democracy. She promises that she will 'Never use the word "subject". Instead [she will] use the word "participant" ', and 'include data about myself in the research, as one of the participants', as if equality between subjects and psychologists was simply a matter of presenting more data and using more liberal words (1986: 29). Such a vague definition of democracy, which does not recognize the unequal power of psychologists and subjects, gives woman-centred methods a potential for authoritarianism. Since one woman is the equal of any other, woman-centred psychologists can claim the right to represent the rest. Any self-declared woman-centred account or interpretation of experience can assume the status of absolute truth. Anecdotes may become the basis of entire theories, as in Eichenbaum and Orbach's (1982) work.

Woman-centred methods restrict feminist psychology in other ways. They tend to treat language as an unproblematic expression of women's experience, and they are too directed by the need for feminist change to do justice to the unconscious. Douglas suggests that the Women's Liberation Movement might find similarities between the 'unconscious elements' she discovers in her research interviews, and consciousness-raising (1986: 30). The emphasis of woman-centred methods on particular ways of articulating personal experience also makes it highly socially specific, but it rarely recognizes this. Douglas even wants to 'forget about selecting samples and controlling variables' (1986: 29). She suggests no further analysis of power differences between subjects. She seems to think deliberate amnesia can take care of them.

Woman-centred psychology, like egalitarian feminist psychology, needs to address theory if it is really to change psychological discourses of gender. Often, it deploys explanatory frameworks taken from traditional and egalitarian feminist psychology. Miller (1976) draws on learning theory, describing men as socialized into separation and mastery, and women into emotional connection and, negatively, subjugation. Eichenbaum and Orbach (1982) also see women's socialization as producing characteristic concerns with connection and emotion. Ernst and Goodison (1981) draw a mixture of Gestalt, Reichean, psychodrama, transactional analysis, and other self-help therapeutic theories into feminist therapeutic explanations. Jungianism is particularly influential in woman-centred psychological theory. Its negative descriptions of femininity are ignored or upgraded (e.g. Cox 1981), but not restructured; and its racist assumptions are rarely scrutinized.

Egalitarian feminists reject the idealizations and homogenizations which they think woman-centred feminist theories of subjectivity involve. Rowbotham *et al.* criticize the feminists who assume that 'under a "false" non-feminist consciousness sits a "true" natural feminism in every woman' (1979: 105). Egalitarian feminist psychologists like Deaux (1976), Unger (1979), and Henley (1985) make similar criticisms. Even Baumrind (1982), supporting Gilligan's different voice hypothesis against what she sees as the traditionalism of the psychology of androgyny, holds on to the traditional framework of Jungian psychology in order to do this, and later (1986), reinterprets the hypothesis in a humanist and spiritual framework, which is not differentiated by gender. But egalitarian feminists' dependency on traditional psychological theory means that they often reproduce its limited formulations of subjectivity and gender. To some feminist psychologists, a gynocentric theory seems a better response (Wine 1985).

Woman-centred feminism often neglects theory in favour of documenting feminine experience. Where it does develop theories, it tends to found them on a specifically female individual consciousness, assuming that, if we learn to think and feel gynocentrically, we can overcome patriarchy. It is here, as much as in psychology, that woman-centred theories of subjectivity are articulated; for woman-centred theories look like humanist psychological theories which have redefined human potential as feminine potential. Their origins in North America in the decade after the explosion of the human potential movement helps explain this. They experience all the problems of humanist psychological theories, too. Their psychological, rational concept of the subject allows them to suppose, optimistically, that the contradictions between psychology and social relations can be resolved simply by redefining consciousness. Greer, for instance, aims to produce change by 'bending and selecting' the meanings of male psychologists' words: 'What else can they be for? We cannot allow them to define what must be' (1971: 111). The theories' emphasis on consciousness restricts their ability to deal with other non-psychological differences between subjects, and even undermines the concept of a specifically feminine consciousness which they are interested in. Finally, by trying for an ultimately rational understanding of subjectivity, the theories reduce unconscious aspects of subjectivity to promising problems, which can be overcome. Haug (1987) suggests that if women took a self-conscious and directed approach to their daydreams, these daydreams could be more feminist.

Woman-centred theory also repeats, in more explicit and intense forms, the biologism of humanist psychological theory. In the last instance, it views feminist politics as an elaboration of biology. Daly, in a reduction of culture to biology which recalls Dawkins, says that relations between the sexes are 'subject to evolutionary change' (1970: 145). She invests women's social commonalities with a genetic yet mystical significance, and turns feminism into a kind of club, within which true believers heap praise on each other and vilify the fake women outside. Woman-centred theory's biologism encourages it, again, to neglect differences apart from gender. Morgan describes women's means of communicating and campaigning as universally feminine, 'much more *natural* to them [black, brown and white women] than the very *machismo* style of male-dominated organisations, black, brown *and* white' (1970: xxvi). Lesbianism, too, is often described as a correlate of biology. Rich (1980) appropriates Dinnerstein's and Chodorow's accounts of the construction of femininity through mothering, for a biological theory of a lesbian continuum affecting all women's relations with each other, and succoured by the emotional ties between mothers and daughters. Others postulate a biological, but not reproductive, lesbian identity, which has the potential to reshape kinship relations' current domination by reproduction (Bristow and Pearn 1984, Darty and Potter 1984; see also Zimmerman 1984, Dominy 1986).

Sometimes, woman-centred theory is given a utilitarian justification. This happens especially often with feminists who have a generally egalitarian perspective. Rowbotham *et al.* think feminism has to provide a unified, positive alternative for all women, in order for them to be able not only to know about but to reject and try to escape subordination (1979: 129). But utilitarianism is not enough to sustain woman-centred feminism's more dramatic ambitions.

In psychology, as in woman-centred feminism generally, theory is mainly hijacked from humanist psychology. Miller (1976), for example, links psychological wholeness with a female-identified ability to be concerned with relationships and feelings, as well as logic and achievement. Humanist psychology's familiarity to egalitarian feminist psychologists makes the division between humanist egalitarian, and woman-centred, theories difficult to draw. The most controversial case of this is Gilligan's humanist call for the integration of 'feminine' and 'masculine' perspectives in psychological theory, which is often read as implying the essential rather than the social femaleness of the different voice, and, more broadly, the need for a separate or separatist, gynocentric psychology.[3] As Auerbach *et al*. point out, 'although [Gilligan's] *ultimate* goal is the integration of female and male voices, her emphasis falls on *difference*' (1985: 154). Gilligan gives no examples of cross-gender use of different or traditional voices. The integration of the two voices which she calls for, leaves men with much further to go than women, who she seems to see as already 'bilingual' in moral judgements to some extent (Auerbach *et al*. 1985). She appears to appropriate traditional humanist interests in social connectedness and caring specifically for women. She mentions Chodorow's socialization theory of the transfer of concerns with care and responsibility from mothers to daughters, but she does not make it an integral part of her own account. She recognizes, but does not explore, the different female voice's lack of power. Her fidelity to Kohlberg's approach suggests a maturational framework. And so the different voice can easily be understood as intrinsically, biologically, feminine. As Lott rhetorically asks, if social circumstances do not produce it, 'then from what other source' does it come? (1985: 51).

Woman-centred psychology's humanism tends to reduce the world to a scaled-up version of a subject's psychic conflicts and commitments. Femininity itself remains psychologized, and its traditional connotations may also reappear. Sometimes Gilligan, for instance, seems, against her expressed intention, to resurrect a very old discourse of feminine subjectivity — Patmore's Victorian ideal of women as the domesticated moral conscience of the community, 'the angel in the house'. Defining consciousness in humanist terms means that other social relations also get psychologized or ignored. Orbach and Eichenbaum's work, for example, concentrates on 'splitting' explanations of women's conflicts between family and work commitments, and on models of mother-daughter symbioses within nuclear families. Black feminist psychologists' descriptions of the family as a site of refuge and resistance for black women have no place in this framework. White working-class and black women's stories of employment difficulties and success are heard as case histories of psychic tension, and lesbian women's attempts to redefine relations between women become assimilated to accounts of pre-oedipal intimacy. Gender relations themselves can get passed over in favour of a purely psychological idea of femininity; this generates the conflation between humanism and woman-centredness in Miller's and Gilligan's work. Woman-centred psychology needs a more complex, specific theory.

Like egalitarian feminist psychology, woman-centred psychology sees the gendered subject as both a product of social relations, and a fixed, essential entity. But it leans much more towards the second account. As in woman-centred feminism generally, it finally assimilates its humanist ideas of feminine consciousness to a concept of a biologically feminine subject. Sometimes it associates this biological femininity with sexuality. Sherfey suggests that 'women may possess a *biologically determined*, inordinately high, cyclic sexual drive' (1970: 251) whose suppression is the condition for western social organization. More frequently, reproduction is set up as the foundation of feminine psychology. Sherfey thinks women need to be in closer touch with their life purpose of caring for the species. Cox (1981) is interested in what women's subjectivity may tell us about matriarchal modes of consciousness. Other theories seem to subscribe to cultural rather than biological essentialism. Miller suggests that positive 'feminine' psychic characteristics are socialized away in men, but are ignored and even encouraged in women. Eichenbaum and Orbach share this supposition. But these theories' notions of culturally stable femininity often elide with their concept of a biologically stable individual.

The biological aspect of woman-centred psychological theories provides them with some theoretical distinctiveness. But it also tends to recapitulate mainstream psychological theories of gender, which focus on female subjects' sexual and reproductive difference, and reduce questions about gender, finally, to the need to find out the truth about the biologically sexed subject. Its deterministic view of 'femininity' and 'masculinity' offers no possibility of combining feminine social concern and caring, and masculine logic and individualism, let alone challenging the gendered distinction they derive from. Biological versions of woman-centred psychology also tend, even more than woman-centred feminism generally, to skate over social differences. Even their acknowledgement of differences in sexuality is diluted by their desexualizing assimilation of lesbianism to cultural or biological ideals of femininity.

As in woman-centred feminism generally, woman-centred psychology often defends itself as an effective, rather than a theoretically rigorous, means of resistance, and makes theory a utilitarian adjunct to this aim. Aitkenhead (1987) sees research on women as a way to start tackling men's greater power in psychology. Douglas (1986) simply wants her work to be valuable. But such utilitarian arguments compromise the specificity of woman-centred psychology's aims. Often, too, they echo conventional psychological priorities. Since Douglas does not deal with the questions of *what* is valuable for women, and whether it is valuable for all women, it is likely that the usual socially-biased criteria or psychological worth will be read into the vacuum of her definition.

Woman-centred psychology reminds feminist psychologists of the power of psychological concepts of gender, and acts as a strong inducement to them to challenge these concepts. But it replicates egalitarian feminist psychology's over-attachment to certainty, and to closed, self-sufficient explanatory systems. Its definitions of femininity as at the same time an artefact and an essence are blatantly incompatible, and its attempts to account for all aspects of subjectivity in terms of fixed gender categories, inadequate. These shortcomings can induce practical and theoretical stasis in feminist psychology.

Chapter six

The unconscious and discourse

What seems to me to need attention is . . . [the] movement of psychoanalysis away from content (pre-Oedipal or otherwise) to a concept of sexuality as caught up in the register of demand and desire.
(Rose 1978: 19)

Theoretically, we have now moved beyond psychoanalysis to a position in which the workings of desire are produced through power relations, though the relationship is not a reductive one.
(Urwin in Henriques *et al*. 1984: 322)

Egalitarian and woman-centred feminist psychologies usually assume the rationality and unity of the psychological subject. But some feminist psychologists realise that the subjective experience of gender is not an entirely logical or consistent affair. What do women get out of staying in situations that seem to be against their interests? Do men lose as well as gain from dominant discourses of gender? This chapter examines how feminist psychologists address such questions by using psychoanalytic theories of unconscious subjectivity, and Foucauldian accounts of the discursive construction of conscious and unconscious subjectivities; and how, in the process, they challenge the conventional psychological concept of the subject.

Canguilhem (1980) proposes that psychology should submit its implicit idea of 'man', the psychological subject, to questioning by philosophy. Twentieth-century western philosophers have often addressed psychology (e.g. Toulmin 1953, Habermas 1978, Farrell 1981). Sometimes they even cast doubt on psychology's concept of a logical, autonomous subject, as Chapter 7 describes. But their own preoccupations with rational, thinking subjects often bring them too close to psychology's notion of the subject for them to question it. The psychoanalytic idea of the subject as unconscious, as well as conscious, provides a stronger challenge.

Freud describes the unconscious subject as fragmented and illogical, yet with its own structures and mechanisms.[1] This allows psychoanalysis to address the contradictions of subjectivity, including gendered subjectivity, in a way which other psychological discourses cannot. Psychoanalysis also describes the unconscious as a bisexual or polymorphously sexual force, and maps out the social production and containment of conscious and unconscious sexualities around sexual difference. It tries to explain how it is that 'when you meet a human being, the first distinction you make is, "male or female?" and you are accustomed to making the distinction with unhesitating certainty' (Freud 1933: 113). This lets it challenge psychology's notions of the basically asexual nature of subjectivity, and of the fixity of female and male sexuality. But psychoanalysis's focus on sexual differentiation still often manages to make female-male psychological differences seem absolute. As in psychology generally, femininity and masculinity become psychological and even biological essences. Femininity is painted as a deviant, mysterious, finally unknowable object of investigation, and the 'riddle' of it (Freud 1933: 113) comes to stand for unconscious sexuality as a whole.

Conventional experimental psychology disapproves of the methodological and theoretical uncertainty which the psychoanalytic concept of the unconscious involves (Eysenck 1973, Kline 1981). Humanist psychology, although it is interested in unconscious phenomena, tends to focus on the mechanisms and structures which psychoanalysis proposes, making the unconscious rational, and usurping psychoanalytic insights for itself. Psychology also resists psychoanalysis's centring on sexuality. The discipline has played a part in studies of sexuality since the nineteenth century, when it contributed to scientific and popular debate about the biological and social determination of sexual behaviours. It delineated permitted forms of sexuality, such as those directed towards economically necessary levels of reproduction, and it regulated sexualities which exceeded these limits. It also helped to keep condemned forms of sexuality alive by its perpetual writing and talking about them. Even today, psychological discourses inevitably deal with sexuality, and the emotions and irrationality connected with it, at the same time as they try to ignore it. But psychoanalysis is much more able to discuss prohibited forms of sexuality without pathologizing them, and to describe sexuality as a matter of pleasure, dissociated from biological or social use.

Most contemporary western feminists show some concern with psychoanalysis. Usually they criticize its culture-bound sexism. But they are interested in the subversive power of unconscious sexuality, recognize the explanatory value of unconscious processes, and see psychoanalytic descriptions of psychosexual development as contributions to socialization accounts of dominant gender roles. Friedan condemns Freud's account of women on the grounds that he was a 'prisoner of his own culture' (1965: 93), and criticizes psychoanalytic attempts to explain women's position in terms of a natural feminine sexuality. But she suggests that psychoanalysis's contribution to freeing sexuality is valuable for feminism. Firestone takes Freud's pansexuality as an ideal, and is interested in psychoanalytic accounts of how unconscious mechanisms operate in families. She even calls Freudianism 'the misguided feminism' (1971: 46). Rowbotham ironically defends Freud from over-zealous criticisms of his cultural limitations: 'It didn't occur to [Freud] to criticize the economic basis of competitive capitalism.' And she gives a complex, psychoanalytically-influenced account of her male identification and its effects: 'I had . . . contributed towards making an object of myself and other women. I was partly responsible for our degradation' (1973: 8, 41). She is even able to understand the apparently irrational, masochistic aspects of women's psychology, by drawing on de Beauvoir's implicitly psychoanalytic account of its power: 'Woman assumes her most delicious triumphs by first falling into the depths of abjection . . . the little girl takes delight in a masochism that promises supreme conquests' (de Beauvoir, quoted in Rowbotham 1973: 42).

Psychoanalysis's incompatibility with many aspects of feminism has led contemporary western feminists to be selective in their use of it. Campbell (1987) invokes unconscious mechanisms, such as displacement and projection, to explain specific problems, like conservative women's apparently illogical investment in party structures which withhold power from them. But she does not consider the unconscious as psychoanalysis portrays it, as an enduring, ubiquitous phenomenon which might resist feminist change more generally. Woman-centred feminists such as Rich (1977), deploy psychoanalytic ideas about the importance and persistence of the pre-oedipal relationship between mothers and daughters, but reject the significance psychoanalysis places on women's lack of the phallus. Some feminists pass over Freud's contributions for a more Kleinian-influenced account of motherhood as the primary determinant of psychosexual development (e.g. Chodorow 1978, Chernin 1986), or for a North American psychoanalytic preoccupation with finding compromises between individual, instinctual needs, and social demands (e.g. Gardiner 1987). Feminists also use psychoanalysis to try to understand their links with lesbian and gay, black, and white working-class resistance, about which psychoanalysis itself says little.[2]

Sometimes, feminists reproduce psychoanalysis's own phallocentrism. Greer, for instance, argues that women are socially 'castrated' into a libido-less femininity (1971: 69). Feminists also often use psychoanalysis to idealize sexuality. Firestone displays a Marcusian conviction of the revolutionary effects of the lifting of sexual repression. She presents a vague definition of feminism's final goal as 'Sexual freedom, love, etc' (1971: 271). Greer too invokes Marcuse, and elevates the pursuit of pleasure to a revolutionary tactic: 'The surest guide to the correctness of the path that women take is *joy in the struggle*' (1971: 330). Rowbotham (1973) feels that if she had read Reich earlier, life would have been easier. Like Reich, she thinks that the orgasm 'show[s] a remarkable ability to go its own way' (1973: 55), and resists capitalism and sexism. These writers want to free the disruptive potential of sexual and other pleasures, by lifting their traditional repressions. The reactive character of such arguments can make western feminism priggish, rather than liberating. It means that feminists are liable to retain sexual prohibitions, as well as flouting them. Recent British and US feminist debates about lesbian sado-masochism expressed this prurience (e.g. Califia 1980, Ardill and O'Sullivan 1986). Censured behaviours or attitudes were consistently contrasted with liberatory complements. If censure was directed at non-consent, consensual sexual activity was idealized. If, on the other hand, censure was applied to all physical and psychological domination, a psychologically egalitarian sexuality became the ideal form. In the end, where it was necessary to decide compromises, with such issues as who could use women's and lesbian and gay centres, behaviours often had to be allocated the moral high ground on highly pragmatic criteria: that they were private, or that they didn't involve conspicuous clothing, for instance.

Feminists also tend to diminish the significance of the unconscious, a move which encourages a purely psychological view of the subject. Like many ego psychologists, Greer, for example, sees narcissism as a matter of conscious self-esteem and 'egotism' and views women's defects as concentrated in this psychological area. Rowbotham accepts without criticism Horney's reduction of the unconscious to basic needs, which presupposes a psychological subject of those needs. Campbell (1987) also assumes a fundamental, active, human subject. Following Winship, she relates women's feelings of powerlessness not to unconscious conflicts, but to their ability actively to subordinate themselves. Psychoanalytically-influenced woman-centred feminism identifies this psychological subject specifically with femininity. Rich (1977) sees the meaning of mother-daughter relations, not as unconscious and individual, but as available to any aware female subject. Such psychologistic interpretations of the unconscious tend, like psychoanalysis itself, to gloss over gender and other social relations. Firestone, for instance, associates sexuality with an absolute, ungendered, human essence. She sees racism as a sexual phenomenon in which black women and men are children in an oedipal situation with their white parents, and her romanticization of working-class and black sexuality echoes Freud's own ideas about 'primitiveness': 'Sexually . . . too, ghetto kids are freer' (1971: 115). More subtly, Gardiner (1987) argues for the cultural and historical flexibility of the contents, but not the structure, of what Kohut calls the self-object.

Feminist psychologists are often reluctant to call on psychoanalysis. Maccoby and Jacklin (1974) refuse to consider the psychoanalytically-influenced hypothesis that women's low scores might be due to strong but repressed, rather than weak, aggression, because the first of these is not susceptible to traditional psychological testing. But feminist psychologists are more interested in psychoanalysis than traditional psychologists are, particularly where, as in Horney's work, it acquires a social orientation. Chodorow (1978) and Dinnerstein (1976) use psychoanalysis to provide a detailed account of how gendered subjectivities develop through unconscious socialization in the nuclear family. Some feminist psychologists try to develop the British object relations and North American ego psychological traditions to deal with specific problems like eating disorders and mother-daughter relations (Orbach 1978, Eichenbaum and Orbach 1982, Ernst and Goodison 1981).

Feminist psychologists' interpretation of psychoanalysis tend, again, to simplify away the challenges it presents. Chodorow's assumption of a unified psychological subject on which socialization processes act, diminishes the distinctive irrationality and uncertainty of the psychoanalytic unconscious. The assumption also restricts Chodorow's analysis of social relations. It is, as Adams says,

> what Chodorow retains of the psychical that makes it impossible for her to consider *social relations* in any but the most simplistic way. By conferring the status of unquestionable truth on some aspects of the parent's relation to the infant, she narrows the domain within

which the social can have effects.

(Adams 1983: 51)

Gilligan repeats this problem when she parcels up the unconscious and sexuality in a bundle with carer-infant relations, and deals with it by labelling it 'Chodorow'. Orbach and Eichenbaum similarly reduce unconscious repression to a surmountable obstacle, or, at best, to a supplementary resource, in their therapeutic attempts to increase women's happiness and effectiveness. Lipschitz notes that 'while feminist therapists can attempt the abolition of inhibition in empowering practices, they cannot abolish repression . . . to suggest this is to abolish the unconscious' (1978: 29).

The connections between theories of unconscious subjectivity and feminist politics, which, Lipschitz suggests, might break the feminist therapeutic impasse, have not been spelled out by feminist therapists, or by feminist psychologists more generally. They tend instead to translate the power of gender and other social relations directly into the unconscious. Sometimes they assume that such relations can be altered by intervening at this purely psychological level. Unger (1979) believes that increasing knowledge of harmful unconscious sex-specific processes can help create a sex-neutral society, for example. But she does not discuss how knowledge of these individual processes can translate into social action, nor, more fundamentally, how the unconscious can be made conscious. Alternatively, feminist psychologists' reduction of gender relations to the unconscious makes them see them as irrevocable. Spector Person (1980), for instance, discusses pessimistically how sexuality is a culture-specific but highly determined and largely unconscious basis of identity.

Western feminists like Mitchell (1974) have used Lacanian reformulations of psychoanalysis to reiterate the irrational, sexual nature of the unconscious, and to make psychoanalysis's place in feminism a more important and challenging one. Such work is starting to have an effect in feminist psychology, but it has already had a great influence on feminism. This influence derives primarily from Lacanian psychoanalysis's emphasis on language, a social object which connects strongly with feminist interests in the social nature of gender relations. Lacan adopts Saussurean structuralist linguistics' view of language as a system of oppositions and differences. In such a system, visual and auditory linguistic signifiers are in changing, unstable correspondence with the concepts they stand for. A signifier can never be fixed to a particular concept. Its meaning is defined by its place within the network of signifiers and signifieds: by its differences from the others, and by what it excludes. In order to use language, fixed meanings must be assumed. But perfect understanding or communication of meaning is impossible. Symbol systems, of which language is the most powerful, play a very important part in the structure and development of gender and other social relations. But social relations themselves can also be seen as structured in a symbolic way. Lévi-Strauss's analysis of kinship structures as symbol systems in which female objects of exchange act as signifiers has been the most influential extension of structuralist linguistic analysis into this field.

Lacan transposes these structuralist accounts to the level of individual psychosexual development. In traditional psychoanalysis, the paternal prohibition of oedipal sexuality ends the close relationship between the child and mother; enforces the child's recognition of sexual difference, that is, its recognition of the absence of the phallus from the female body; and introduces it into a wider social world. The sexuality which is forbidden is unknown. Once recognized, it gives rise to the unfulfillable desires which constitute the unconscious. For Lacan, oedipal prohibition is achieved through the 'Nom', which in French is both the 'Name' and homophonically the 'No' of the father. This Name itself becomes the mark of unknowable sexual difference and desire, and generates an unconscious, repressed chain of signifiers with no signifieds. The unconscious's structure is therefore, as Lacan (1977) says, like that of a language, but not the same as one. Yet all other symbol systems are founded on this chain of signifiers.

The Name of the Father moves the child away from imaginary, fantastic representations of the world, where signifiers and signifieds correspond exactly, into the symbolic order, where gaps always exist between signifiers, between signifieds, and between these two levels. The imaginary exists within language, and the symbolic order characterizes non-linguistic signification, so there are no absolute chronological or structural divisions between the two orders. But for Lacan, the unconscious exists in the failures of communication which the symbolic order involves. This account revokes the tendency of psychoanalysis to slide into an ego psychology, which equates the unconscious with the id, and treats it as an interesting but manageable phenomenon, the stuff on which the profession's skill is demonstrated. Lacan emphasizes that the unconscious plays a part in the ego, as well as the id. It is a perpetual influence on every area of psychic life. And since it is an evolving language, always changing its expressions, it is also a continually disruptive influence.

A number of political and cultural theorists have deployed Lacanian ideas to produce accounts of the generation and interpellation of the subject within social relations.[3] But feminists' preoccupation with subjectivity has made them particularly interested in Lacanianism. Some, responding to the phallocentrism which Lacanianism retains from traditional psychoanalysis, try to turn it into a gynocentric psychoanalysis. Irigaray (1985) rejects Lacan's relational account of sexual difference, in which femininity is everything that the Name of the Father, and language itself, does not express. She sees women as excluded from language by their own nature, rather than by masculinity, and interprets this positively, as a concomitant of their pleasurable immuring in their bodies. She makes a sexuality which is dispersed all over these bodies, and which is intimately linked with fluid flow and self-touch, the embodiment of the female psyche. Kristeva (1980) proposes that the pre-oedipal closeness between mothers and children is gendered through sign systems. Women are repressed, she suggests, by their social confinement to a non-arbitrary, rhythmic, semiotic order, which is pre-oedipal. This denigrated order is highly creative and productive, and women's closeness to each other persists within it. It is not exclusively female, but Kristeva dwells on its cultural femininity, and this brings her close to Irigaray's essentialism. Such approaches also support particularly obvious forms of Eurocentrism. Kristeva's account of Chinese women, for instance, is self-conscious about its naming of the 'Other', but still often slips into romantic generalizations (Spivak 1981). But they have stimulated more complex understandings of gender relations in other fields, such as literary theory. And in France, Irigarayan psychoanalysts attained a degree of visibility which led them to appear, for a short period and to some people, as the whole French women's liberation movement (Turkle 1979, Moi 1987).

Other feminists, like Mitchell (1974) and Coward (e.g. Coward and Ellis 1977), have tried to tie Lacanian psychoanalysis to social relations, by interpreting it as a descriptive account of how discourses of femininity and masculinity are reproduced, through language, in our conscious and unconscious subjectivities. As with Lacan's own work, these readings see femininity and masculinity as defining each other. Masculinity implies the femininity it excludes. Both terms are representations of, but not solutions to, the problem of what constitutes sexual difference. Rose, rereading Freud's Dora case history, interprets the woman's hysteria as signifying, through its silence, not a feminine denial of sexual difference, but the desire which is the insoluble, unrepresentable '*question* of sexual difference' (1978: 18). The value attached to this question, and the usual psychoanalytic answer to it, are seen by many feminists as completely or largely socially determined. These social readings of Lacanian psychoanalysis have allowed feminist literary, film, and cultural studies to refine their simplistic descriptions of subjectivity on the basis of biological sex or social gender relations. As Kaplan says, feminists 'understand femininity and masculinity in a psychoanalytic sense as descriptive terms that no individual psychic or social subject can actually embody'. In her case, this lets her make 'better sense of symbolic narratives' (1986: 11).[4] Lacanian concepts of signifers, desire, and the Imaginary, have become common feminist currency. Some feminists have also used Lacanian psychoanalysis to try to make marxist theories of class take gender and subjectivity more seriously, and have attempted integrated accounts of these different areas of experience.[5] Feminists have used Lacanian ideas to extend their specific understandings of differences other than gender. The relationship between signification and subjectivity is very important for some feminist considerations of 'race' and class (e.g. Spivak 1981, Steedman 1986).

What does Lacanian psychoanalysis offer to feminist psychologists? It challenges conventional psychology's idea of a unified, stably gendered subject, by offering an analysis of how gendered subjects are produced in and through symbol systems. It implies that, since subjects cannot completely understand or communicate with each other, or even themselves, the full 'representation' of women by female subjects, or of particular, female-identified subject areas, methods or theories, is impossible. It also offers one way in which feminist psychologists can develop the interdisciplinary connections which interest them: by exploring, in common with other workers across the social sciences and humanities, unconscious significations.

So far, Lacanian psychoanalysis has been neglected by psychologists. In Britain, Clifford and Frosh (1982) proposed that a Lacanian-informed approach to the psychology of interpersonal relationships, development, and irrationality, would avoid the traditional discipline's obsession with single, uncontradictory meanings. This was not taken up by mainstream researchers. Lacanianism has allowed some feminist psychologists to intensify their awareness of the complex psychic structures and process psychoanalysis deals with, and of the sophistication of psychoanalytic explanations. Sayers (1986), for instance, describes psychological and traditional and Lacanian psychoanalytic theories of sexual difference, and their implications for feminism. But she does not aim to address psychological issues outside the psychoanalytic field. Adams's response to Chodorow's ego psychology provides a Lacanian account of 'the constitution of a split subject through the play of presence and absence' (1983: 47). But it, too, addresses itself much more to feminism than to psychology. And even though Sayers and Adams are psychologists, their work is only recognizable as psychology by a very few feminist psychologists. Apart from such work, Lacanian psychoanalysis has been ignored by feminist psychologists. This is partly because, like most psychologists, they find the unconscious difficult to cope with. But Lacanian psychoanalysis's lack of impact also results more specifically from its interest in the complexities of language and other signification systems. Feminist psychologists, like other psychologists, usually take a more straightforward approach to language.

Psychology underplays the part that language plays in its investigations. It treats it as a specific object of investigation, or else ignores it. Language is acquiring increased visibility in the field of cognitive science. Social psychology is more and more interested in linguistic and ethnographic methods, and in the analysis of linguistic social representations, accounts, and repertoires. But most of these approaches still see signifiers as expressing meanings directly, a few or even one at a time; and therefore as being susceptible, despite their complications, to rational, more or less complete analyses. In feminism, the same is often true. Some feminists also idealize symbol systems, as arenas of unproblematic female community: 'laughter is a form of communication which is understood by both of us', Hobson, a middle-class researcher, writes, of her interview with a working-class housewife (1981: 82). Woman-centred feminists like Daly (1979) do not bother with such defensive explanations, but get on with building a female language. Nevertheless, feminists recognize that women's exclusion from culture and language is an important aspect of their experiences of subordination. And they realize the power of names to define subjectivity, reduce opposition to manageable levels, and induce paralysis.[6]

Feminist psychological studies of language concentrate on the effects of words with sex-typed associations; on whether women and men understand, use and develop language as a whole very differently; and on whether the language of an investigation affects the results.[7] Feminists working on social representations recognize, in addition, that human experience is highly symbol dependent, that the issue of language can usefully link psychology with other work in the social sciences and humanities, and that a greater focus on this area might be useful for psychological investigations of many gender issues (e.g. Wetherell *et al.* 1987). Like other researchers on social representations, however, they often psychologize these representations. They see them as a modulation of other cognitive patterns, and as a realm parallel to the realm of gender relations, and determined by it in a fairly direct way. In all these approaches, influences on language other than gender are skated over. Lakoff (1975) mentions cultural similarities in patterns of women's and men's language use, and proposes that feminists should learn from the black consciousness movement's pride in Black English, but she does not extend this awareness into an analysis of differences within women's and men's languages.

Lacanian-influenced feminism is hardly an ideal response to the deficiencies in feminist psychology. Numerous criticisms have been directed at it from inside[8] and outside feminism. Does attention to unconscious wishes and conflicts necessarily produce a more careful gender politics? Mightn't it merely give rise to a new, psychologistic, feminist reductionism? Isn't the truth of Canguilhem's claim that philosophy is on 'the side of the people and of the born non-specialists' (1980: 49), even more debatable, when it is applied to psychoanalysis of any kind? Doesn't a psychoanalytically-influenced feminism depend ultimately, like psychoanalysis itself, on the professional authority of discoveries made in the analytic session, by analysts who are, in any case, rarely feminists? And most importantly, aren't Lacanian feminist explanations retreats from feminist politics, into psychoanalysis's traditional phallocentrism?

Like other forms of psychology, psychoanalysis tends to produce an idealized discourse of the subject. In psychoanalysis, though, this discourse focuses on unconscious sexuality. The untestability and undecidability of the unconscious is absolutized, making 'the unconscious' a catch-all explanatory category. And since the unconscious can be approached most nearly through unmeasurable, unrepeatable events in the analytic situation, psychoanalysts, even more than other psychologists, retain for themselves the power of being the only subjects able to explain subjectivity. Lacanian psychoanalysis's new theoretical language, and its interest in the intrinsic difficulties of language, intensifies this expert authority. A similar hegemonic expertise characterizes feminist Lacanians. The detailed analyses they make of unconscious significations can stop them from considering any other kind of explanation. The unconscious may take on the status of an answer to everything: a last piece of the jigsaw, which feminists initiated into Lacanianism can use to solve the issue on another plane, or can reject. Alternatively, textual expressions of the unconscious are made the centre of analysis, generating affirmations of textual-sexual pleasure which often recall those produced by non-psychoanalytic, woman-centred work. Irigaray and Kristeva both provide good examples, their idealizations of feminine desire overriding the difference between Irigaray's conflation of feminine desire and lesbianism, and Kristeva's determined separation of the two. Such idealizations lose the sense of impossible desire on which Rose insists.

Lacanianism has little interest in the links between unconscious signification, and social and historical relations. Like psychotherapy, it places itself outside these relations. This presents further problems for feminism. The feminist commitment to changing gender relations demands that such relationships should be explored. But, as Kaplan notes of Mitchell, feminist Lacanians tend to assimilate the linguistic unconscious to ideology, and to leave ideology's relation to the material world unclear. It is this elision that sometimes brings feminist Lacanians to echo the traditional gendered and even androcentric nature of the psychoanalytic unconscious. Mitchell emphasizes the variability displayed in the psychological and social marking of sexual difference. But she argues that, because this marking is universal, it is probably inevitable. She also suggests that, because sexual difference is always expressed phallocentrically in social relations, phallocentrism too may be inevitable. Kaplan, more cautiously, views certain psychic elements as stabler than others, but she too stresses 'the persistence of psychic structure in relation to the shifting social elements of psychic content' (1986: 11).

Where feminist Lacanianism is more socially oriented, the unconscious tends to be reduced to an artefact of social relations. Language becomes an essentialized mediator between social relations and the unconscious. Coward and Ellis (1977), for instance, criticize the notion of signification as part of an ideological cloud formation above the real economic and political world, and assert its materiality; but its relationship to other aspects of the material world remains unclear. Coward and Ellis also try to challenge the traditional concept of the individual, psychological subject, by analysing the existence of this subject in and through language. But this is not enough to deal with the multiple expressions and experiences of subjectivity.[9]

Canguilhem believes that the interrogation of psychology by philosophy which he proposes has important consequences:

Once in a while at least, the philosopher must be allowed to approach the psychologist as a counsellor and to say: if you leave the Sorbonne by the exit in the Rue Saint-Jacques, you can either turn up the hill or go down towards the river: if you go up, you will get to the Panthéon which is the resting place of a few great men, but if you go downhill then you're bound to end up at the Préfecture de Police.

(Canguilhem 1980: 49)

Psychoanalysis's relationship to psychology could be seen in a similar way. A psychology that ignores it is more likely to turn into a dogmatic police force of a discourse. Feminist psychologists can, like other psychologists, try to develop a psychology based on conventional ideas of the subject, in order to police subjectivity; or they can deal more fully with the complexities of gendered subjectivity, by using psychoanalysis. But psychoanalysis's limited address to social relations makes it unable to deal with all the questions western feminists raise about gender and subjectivity.

Some feminists are trying to analyse conscious and unconscious subjectivities, not psychoanalytically, but as the products of discourses, structures of knowledge that are embedded in particular historical and social relations of power. For a discipline that generally deals simplistically with social relations, and rarely studies its own or its subjects' histories, such an approach is especially important.[10] It has already been used widely to analyse discourses of objects which interest feminist psychology, including mother-child relations, and biology (Sayers 1982, Riley 1983, Urwin 1985, Walkerdine and Lucey 1989). Such accounts provide detailed and wide-ranging analyses of the psychological and related discourses around these objects. They check feminism's tendency to draw uncritically on psychological explanations. But within psychology, their effects are small. They are directed primarily at feminists, and so they tend to treat conscious and unconscious subjectivities as discursive artefacts, granting them no autonomous analysis. 'What is to be done with the category of "psychology" is another history,' as Riley (1978: 90) says.

Many feminists adopt more variable programmes, which combine analysis of discourses, with an address to the unconscious. Since this approach allows subjectivity to be addressed through the unconscious, it is particularly valuable in psychology. *Changing the Subject* (Henriques *et al.* 1984) is the principal psychological example so far. The book tries to challenge psychology's concept of the subject, both by studying unconscious subjectivity, and by constructing Foucauldian genealogies of discourses of the subject. It analyses the subjects of different areas of psychology, as intersections of discourses of different subjects: medical, legal, state welfare and popular, as well as psychological. Like Canguilhem, Henriques *et al.* view history as a way of understanding the cohesion of psychology's diverse objects, theories and methods around the individual subject. The complex, changing, and often unconscious nature of discourses, the analysis's own discursive positioning, and the differences within it, mean that it cannot reach a complete understanding of psychology's discursive subjects. But through this uncertainty, it aims to keep the concept of the subject in doubt.

Changing the Subject pays continuous attention to psychological, psychoanalytic, and social discourses of gender. Urwin, for example, tries to develop an alternative to individual-centred, gender-indifferent psychology of language development. She deploys a Foucauldian version of Lacanian theory, which suggests that language emerges in and through the recognition of power differences, including gender differences. She notes how a 2-year-old girl surrenders a toy tool box to a boy she is playing with in front of a video observation camera, with the words, '*Boy* have it' (Henriques *et al.* 1984: 317). The words mark both the girl's mastery of sexual difference, and her subjugation by it; both her pleasure in her mastery of an appropriate action, and her lack of social power. Hollway discusses the separation of 'thinking' and 'feeling' in the heterosexual relationships of women and men. Despite the individual histories and contradictions of these relationships, women tend to represent themselves as doing the feeling and men the thinking. Hollway relates the unconscious splitting which these representations indicate, to wider 'split' structures of gender power.

Discourse-oriented feminist psychology runs into some problems. At times, it seems to construct its own new orthodoxies, reproducing those in Foucault's analyses (e.g. 1979). Henriques *et al.*'s binary model of power and its absence is flexible enough to apply to many different kinds of discourses. But uncertainties are smoothed over by this idealization of a historically and socially specific, juridical concept of power (Hussain 1981). The concept makes Foucauldian 'discourse' itself a broad, vague category, and homogenizes analyses of socially and historically distinct discourses. This smoothing over of social and historical differences can turn discourse analyses' political implications from productive ambiguity, to complete opacity. It becomes difficult to see how discourses can change. Adams, for instance, says, of the historical analysis of discourses of 'mothering' she suggests, that 'it is unclear what purchase political action would have' on it (1983: 51). The Foucauldian equation between knowledge and power is left so general that it can be appropriated by the most tenuously 'feminist' of psychologies. It has been adopted as a slogan for assertiveness training programmes for US women managers, for example. This simplification sometimes affects Henriques *et al.*'s versions of Foucauldian genealogies, too. Hollway, focusing on how discourses of gender produce unconscious splits in relationships between women and men, recognizes that these discourses are more socially specific than her account is able to detail. But she undercuts this realization with footnotes which describe similarities, but no differences, in the articulation of gender in homosexual relationships; and which parallel the unconscious splits generated by discourses of gender, with those generated by racist discourses: 'When I made generalisations about women (almost always derogatory), I did not include myself in the group I was talking about. . . . The same phenomenon occurs with colonised people' (Henriques *et al.* 1984: 229, 260).

Henriques *et al.* recognize Foucault's political limits: failure to account for change, and the difficult relationship between discourse and realities (1984: 108–9). They conclude that these difficulties are less important than Foucauldian analyses' ability to address psychology in new ways. But their work gives rise to another problem. Foucault hopes to defuse the concept of the subject by analysing its distribution among discourses of conscious and unconscious subjectivity. Urwin wants to go 'beyond psychoanalysis' (Henriques *et al.* 1984: 321). To do this is also to go 'beyond' the unconscious, and it seems impossible to do this, as Urwin hopes, without reducing the unconscious, the last resort of subjectivity's difficulty, to a discursive product. Subjectivity becomes contained in discourse: a solution which does not deal adequately with its complicated place in psychology and social relations.

It has been argued that Foucault's intense interest in analysing discourses of the human subject (Foucault 1982) allows an unnoticed ideal of subjectivity to persist in his work (Cousins and Hussain 1984). Henriques *et al.* try to use the unconscious to avoid Foucault's simplicity about subjectivity. But sometimes they become too enthusiastic about this, and turn the unconscious into an ideal, a pseudo-subject in its own right. Power relations cannot be addressed if the unconscious is evoked in such an absolute, disconnected way. Hollway, for instance, seems to see splitting as a process working on an original psychic entity, an unconscious subject, whose relations to discourse are left unspecified.

At times, Henriques *et al*. also appear to back out of their theoretical commitment to language. They want to avoid the sterile epistemological debates with which they think language is often involved. And so they follow the pattern of Foucault's less textually-oriented work. Although they recognize that social relations, discourses, and language are not the same thing, their practice tends to belie this. Sometimes they approach language as if it expresses power relations and subjectivity directly, and originates from the very autonomous, fixed subjects whose existence they are challenging. They ignore ambiguities in their own writing, and in their interview material, which they treat as unproblematically quotable. Hollway, for example, quotes a man's description of his split relationship with a woman as 'shrivelled' (Henriques *et al*. 1984: 253). This odd word could have started an analysis of whether discourses of heterosexual relationships are connected to discourses of, perhaps, masculinity, and nature.

Changing the Subject does not always manage to integrate its Lacanian challenge to the concept of the subject, with its Foucauldian challenge to interpretations of historical and social relations. At times, it reproduces the limitations of both. As Henriques *et al*. acknowledge, such problems are probably inevitable. When juggling two radical theories with a commitment to addressing issues important in psychology, something has got to give. Henriques *et al*.'s interest in discursive structure takes them too far from psychology, and their fascination with an absolutely psychological unconscious brings them too close to it for them to be able to pursue feminist and psychological interests together. Their initiative is nevertheless valuable for feminist psychology. Its address to discourse and the unconscious points to important uncertainties, which traditional psychology largely ignores. Such interests are slowly diffusing to other feminist psychologists, who have previously been distanced from them by the constraints of the mainstream discipline.

Chapter seven

Forming associations

. . . regarding individuals and social events from the perspective of feminism as world-view may itself encourage the very tendency to objectify our 'subjects' which feminism opposes so forcefully.

(Condor 1986b: 111–12)

Feminist psychology of women will generate no universal laws, promise no uncomplicated models of change, and offer no easy routes to undermining gender-biased differentials.

(Fine 1985: 180)

Feminist psychology needs to deal with both the questions about the subject which traditional psychology is interested in, and the gender and other power relations which preoccupy feminists, but which traditional psychology neglects. Previous chapters have described a number of initiatives which manage at times to combine these psychological and feminist interests. This chapter will argue that an important aspect of such initiatives is their address to the ambiguous significatory structures of psychological discourse. This turns the analyses into what I shall call 'associative' feminist psychologies. The chapter explores the characteristics and value of associative elements in feminist psychology, and discusses the similarities between them and other critical practices.

Psychological knowledge is unavoidably ambiguous, and this is especially clear when it involves relatively ill-defined, social aspects of subjectivity, like gender. To compensate for this, feminist psychology, like traditional psychology, often becomes excessively systematic. The programmes developed by egalitarian and woman-centred feminist psychologists are manifestations of this over-attachment to certainty. Each is formulated as a closed, self-sufficient system. But each is inadequate for some important feminist psychological concerns. Feminist psychologists are more aware of the ambiguities in psychological discourses than conventional psychologists are, and are increasingly championing heterogeneity, speculation, and uncertainty (e.g. Henley l985). Unger quotes Russell, 'uncertainty in the presence of vivid hopes and fears is painful, but must be endured if we wish to live without the support of fairy tales' (1983: 29). But among feminist researchers and practitioners, these concerns with uncertainty have limited currency. A sustained address to the linguistic and other symbol systems which support and express discourses of the individual subject and of gender might change this. Such structures constitute the written, spoken, and behavioural material of psychology. But they are never complete or self-sufficient. Feminist analyses of them are compelled to co-exist with their uncertainties, and to make links with other, non-psychological discourses, such as discourses of gender.

As the last chapter argued, many feminist psychologists pass over signification, in favour of simpler objects. The few who, influenced by psychoanalysis and poststructuralism, take a more serious approach to it, tend to address it within an orthodox social cognitivist framework, to treat it as an illustration of larger, more obviously social discursive structure, or to ground it finally in an idealized unconscious subjectivity. But elements of a more ambivalent, productive, associative approach to signification also exist within feminist psychology.

Unlike the versions of feminist psychology examined before, associative feminist psychologies are rarely deliberately or self-consciously adopted. Even when their specific characteristics are recognized, they are given different interpretations and names. But it is possible to describe the commonalities between these feminist psychologies, in a way which points up the importance of the associative approach for feminist psychology in general.

Associative feminist psychologies address the different signification systems which make up psychology's material and psychology itself. They work with the variability and contradictoriness of signs, without imposing single meanings on them. They search out associations, not equations. They do this by adopting something like a structuralist understanding of signification systems, treating them as changing structures of oppositions and differences, where obvious meanings are always shadowed by the meanings they exclude. Associative feminist psychologies' commitment to foregrounding secondary, neglected meanings also recalls some poststructuralist projects. Since psychological discourse is centred on a concept of its object as an autonomous and purely psychological subject, its secondary meanings involve unbounded, extrapsychological, social objects. Associative feminist psychologies make unstable, continually changing liaisons with these social objects; and so they are associative in two senses.

Feminist psychologies which work by association, stay close enough to psychology's concerns to be able to contest them. But they also explore psychology's boundaries: an important focus for a discipline so determined to define itself rigorously. Associative feminist psychologies also evade rigid definitions of feminism, and pursue the interdisciplinary, contextual, social interests which feminist psychologists are increasingly developing. Finally, the heterogeneities and instabilities of associative feminist psychologies help them avoid reifying or reducing historically and theoretically important distinctions between symbol systems, and between discourses. In this way, they manage to give a picture of how the structural ambiguities of discourses of gender and the individual subject intersect.

The most obvious level of psychology's ambiguous significations is that of its writing. Psychology is predominantly a written discourse, conducted through the publication of books and papers. The writing is preoccupied with psychology's status and definition as a male-identified objective science. The unknown, unscientific, 'feminine' aspects of subjectivity remain excluded and unwritten. In this way, psychological writing manages to smooth over the difficulties in its discourses of gender. But what you read is not all you get, and what is not on the page is often as important as what is.

By reading between the lines of textual data and other psychological texts, associative feminist psychologies comment on what is written into and out of psychological discourse. Some of the most successful feminist challenges to traditional psychology have worked in this way, accentuating, almost as symptoms, the conflicting psychological meanings of particular words or phrases. Gilligan's work provides good examples. The phrase 'a different voice', which has come to serve as a popular and psychological shorthand for her conclusions, has important but ambivalent significances for psychology and feminism. Gilligan's assertion of a different 'voice' disturbs psychological discourse by its introduction of a modality associated with unwritten, professionally illegitimate knowledge. The different 'voice' is troubling for contemporary western feminism, too, since feminism aims to take account of such voices, but is often accused of silencing or ignoring the less powerful of them. 'Difference' has an ambiguous but central significance in psychology, a discipline whose first concern is testing hypotheses of similarity for differences which are statistically significant. Since the falsification of one hypothesis of similarity leads to the formation and testing of another, these differences are never settled, and so 'difference' is the sign of what psychology does not, as well as of what it does, know. 'Difference' is also an object of frequent feminist debate about the nature of differences between women and men, and of differences between women and between men which interact with these gender-related patterns (Barrett 1987). These double meanings underlie the controversies about the empirical and theoretical status of sex differences, which have developed around Gilligan's work.

Associative feminist psychology also puts the larger-scale written structures of mainstream psychology in question. Psychological writing proclaims itself an abstract, atemporal record of investigations. It aims to avoid non-scientific writing, especially pleasurable, female-identified narrative forms. But these forms remain powerful within psychology. They are especially obvious in feminist psychology, which is always supplementing scientific psychological narrative with stories and examples. Gilligan's work is remembered most through detailed biographical cases, like those of Amy and Jake. Such work makes an association between psychological writing and apparently non-psychological narrative forms, which points up the ubiquitous but usually denied role of these forms in psychological discourses.[1]

Psychological writing generates ambiguities at the level of theory, and associative feminist psychologies stress these uncertainties, too. Bem's challenge to the unchangeability of gender identities, and Gilligan's effort to introduce an ignored theme to psychological theory, for instance, display more acute forms of conventional psychology's oscillation between the concept of an essentially sexed, purely psychological subject, on which it centres, and the concept of a contingently gendered subject. This subject cannot be accounted for completely within psychology, so psychology tries to exclude it; but it keeps intruding in it (Bem 1983, Gilligan 1982, 1986). Gilligan's work also emphasizes psychology's uneasy relationship with male-identified science. Following mainstream psychology's prescriptions, it presents itself as committed to good methodology. At one point, it even adopts the most severe, falsificationist version of traditional method, arguing that any one of its falsifications of the existing psychological theory of moral reasoning should lead that theory to be rejected. But Gilligan also says that she is not interested simply in data, and that her arguments do not depend on the statistical significance of her results. And she uses an eclectic range of procedures, from experiments and questionnaires to semi-structured and counselling interviews. This contradictory fidelity to and departure from methodological rigour undermines the already dubious self-sufficiency of discourses of psychology as a science.

Discourses are not just constituted by what is and is not written; other signification systems are involved. Different symbol systems have different structures, but the commonalities between them allow each to be addressed as patterns of signifiers and signifieds, and discourses to be seen as made up of texts, as well as power relations. This broader approach to signification is particularly important in areas like psychoanalysis and applied psychology, which depend heavily on practices. Such practices involve specific structures of speech, non-verbal communications, and emotional or social functioning, on the part of both practitioners, and clients or patients. As with writing, structures of practice construct meanings, and they do this by what they leave out, as well as what they include. Psychodynamic psychotherapy, for example, is usually oriented around communications, behaviours or emotions which are seen as socially appropriate, such as success in relationships and paid work. These criteria connote reproductive heterosexuality, and male-, middle-class-dominated employment. Non-reproductive sexuality, homosexuality, female sexuality in general, and the temporary, part-time, or unpaid employment which is associated particularly with women, undergo a complementary exclusion. This structure often requires a deliberate effort to maintain. An especially blatant case is the British Psycho-Analytical Society's insistence that homosexuality constitutes grounds for refusing candidates for training. Feminist psychologists have been more aware than others of the ambiguous significations of psychological practices. A Task Force of the APA's Division of the Psychology of Women, for instance, has recognized, as feminists in other social and natural sciences have done, that feminists' position in the mainstream discipline always involves a degree of marginality (Lott 1985). However well-integrated they seem to be, they are still outsiders, as well as insiders, and they have to work with this double agency.

Psychology's concern to present itself as a self-contained discourse means that connections with specific historical and social circumstances, even with other discourses, can in the end play little part in it. In such a defensive yet vulnerable discipline, initiatives which challenge its boundaries by forming explicit links with other discourses, can be particularly valuable for feminism. It is in these cases that the 'associative' character of some feminist psychologies becomes clearest. Gilligan's work intensifies the conflict within Kohlbergian theory, between apparently neutral psychological explanations of, and value-laden extrapsychological prescriptions about, gender (Flanagan 1982). In doing so, it acts as a kind of analysis of this conflict. The analysis is strengthened because the psychology of moral reasoning is close to one particular non-psychological discourse: philosophy, from which it is nevertheless determined to assert its autonomy. Feminist analyses of the interdependence in psychology of biologically and socially gendered subjects, and the excluded, secondary status of the latter, also provide good examples. By linking psychological concepts with their discursive histories, they underline the inadequacies of psychology's ahistorical self-descriptions, and produce an 'association' between psychology as a discourse of the individual, and psychology as social analysis (e.g. Sayers 1982, Henriques *et al.* 1984, Ussher 1989). By describing, for example, the histories of western psychological concepts of the Madonna-like good mother, who is present, sensitive, and, currently, stimulating, and the bad mother, who is the reverse, they map out the political and ideological origins and currencies these concepts have, beyond the biologized significance which traditional psychology gives them (e.g. Adams 1983, Hardyment 1983, Riley 1983, New and David 1985, Urwin 1985). Such analyses are especially important, now that western psychology has acquired wide influence within other discourses and facility in appropriating their key elements, and is trying to extend its academic and applied spheres of influence even further.

The work of black and Third World feminists provides particularly clear examples of associative feminist challenges to psychology's disciplinary boundaries.[2] Although it is often not specifically psychological, such work deals with issues which psychologists, especially feminist psychologists, are interested in. Ladner's (1979) account of young black girls growing up in US cities in the 1960s, for example, was written against conventional sociological accounts of pathological socialization in the black family, and within a black studies perspective. But its opposition to traditional psychological accounts of socialization, and its articulation, against white feminism, of a specific and positive role for the Afro-American family, leads it to be cited by many feminist psychologists, and the first edition of Williams's (1979) *Psychology of Women* reader took it as the sole representative of psychological work about black women in the overdeveloped world.

Ladner relates young black women's subjectivities to the multiple, often conflicting forms of poverty and discrimination in the world they grow up in. She connects psychological variables like parental contact and control, extended family and peer care and contact, the girls' autonomy and responsibility, their hostility and suspicion towards the world, and their early sense of themselves as adult women rather than children, to specific social, political and economic oppressions which affect them. She ignores the usual boundaries drawn between these factors, and subjective experience. She even suggests an explicitly non-psychological change in the work of social and behavioural analysts. They need, she says, to try viewing the black child 'as a more emotionally stable and well integrated personality than his white middle-class counterparts' (1979: 125). Psychology confines its accounts of socialization largely to interpersonal interactions, and, in the 1960s, concentrated on the primary carer. Ladner's work points to the suppressed uneasiness and inadequacies within this approach, by linking young black girls' socialization to the social, economic, and political relations which conventional socialization psychology ignores.

The Heart of the Race (Bryan *et al.* 1985) is a more recent instance of a black feminist text which is not explicitly psychological, but is frequently invoked by feminist psychologists, and works as a kind of associative feminist psychology. It associates black, predominantly Afro-Caribbean, women's experiences with the structure of the British state; analyses the history of their oppression by colonialism and slavery; and grounds their resistant subjectivities in histories of female, family, Afro-Caribbean and African identity. Another recent example is Arguelles's and Rich's description of twentieth-century lesbians' and gay men's lives in Cuba. This study's 'diverse systems of inquiry' include 'historical analysis . . . survey, field and experimental methods', and draw on 'gay scholarship and the politicoeconomic and phenomenological study of Cuban social life' (1984: 685). It both departs from and rejoins traditional and feminist psychologies of homosexuality, which rest on unproblematic notions of homosexual biology, identity, or, more rarely, politics (Kitzinger 1987). It implies that in some circumstances psychology should be associated closely with, for example, political history; but it does not underplay the significance of subjectivity, or 'experience'.

Is a recognition of contradictory yet interdependent, included and excluded meanings enough to provide feminist psychology with a double address to subjectivity and to gender relations? Can such an approach produce change in psychology, or is it confined to exposing the endless subtle differences between signifiers and signifieds? The associative initiatives I have mentioned often produce only small and short-lived changes in feminist psychology, or turn into a recapitulation of one side of an old polarity. Bem's (1983) attempt to dissolve rather than balance gender schemata remains entangled with dominant discourses of sexuality and gender in ways which are difficult to overcome. Gilligan's work, which tries to transcend the gendering of moral values, finally returns to a traditionally feminine set of values. Urwin recognizes that dominant ideas of good motherhood appeal to women's fantasies, but she endorses feminist prescriptiveness about maternity when she pictures these fantasies as mainly pernicious and restricting. Similarly, New and David acknowledge that to be a 'good mother' 'feels enormously powerful and encompassing' (1985: 195), but see this feeling as part of a culture-specific 'myth' of motherhood which can be dispelled by socially shared and supported parenting. Discourse-oriented analyses are particularly likely to jettison psychological discourses' specific interests; they are not really their concern. Ladner's and Bryan *et al.*'s work, which does not even address psychology specifically, provides clear examples.

These analytic shortfalls happen because, although associative initiatives address the ambiguities of subjective meanings, they often end up resolving them by referring to a concept of a unified subject. Because Bem and other gender schema theorists assume that rationality and cognitive unity characterize psychological subjects, they tend to see the break-up of gender schemata as hindered by dominant social relations, but still as fairly straightforward in itself. Because Gilligan assumes that rational subjects are the receptacles of moral values, she underestimates the extent to which the irrational strength of gender continues to influence the values she is trying to recast as simply 'human'. Urwin and New and David revalue the absent, 'bad' mother-subject positively, and ascribe the potential for 'good mothering' more widely than usual, as a capacity of carers other than the mother. But these arguments rest on a belief in a general vocational potential for something like 'good mothering', which they see as fundamentally a property of individuals. They do not question whether this concept of relational potential itself may be generated, as Adams (1983) suggests, within specific discourses of the subject. With Riley (1983), Ladner, and Bryan *et al.*, the situation is different. Such work explicitly brackets off the problematic concept of the psychological subject, and pursues other questions.

The linguistic and other significatory structures of psychological discourse are rare objects of psychological investigation, so simply focusing on them has some critical impact. But associative feminist initiatives also achieve some highly cautious, undramatic discursive shifts, which do not reduce social relations to side-effects of individual subjectivities. I shall argue that it is their particular use of rhetoric that permits this.

All psychological signification involves persuasion, or rhetoric. Associative feminist psychologies' awareness of the ambiguities of psychological signification is also an awareness of the rhetorical figures which structure this signification. This awareness is, itself, achieved through rhetoric. Because rhetoric works on the uncertain relations between signifiers and signifieds, associative feminist psychologies can never produce complete, authoritative accounts of gendered subjectivity. But rhetoric is not an infinitely flexible form of analysis. A rhetorical figure does not disrupt a conventional meaning randomly; it shifts it in a particular direction. And so rhetoric allows associative feminist psychologies to address psychology from outside, but from a recognizable and relevant perspective. Feminist work on androgyny generates paraodic exaggerations of psychology's contradictory methodological allegiances to reliability, and social validity. This parody seems to have encouraged feminist psychologists to extend their understanding of psychology's ambiguities from method, into theory. Gilligan's challenge to the ambiguities of feminism and psychology also uses parody. Her ambivalent adherence to psychology's methodological and narrative standards, and her uncertain characterization of women's different voice, exaggerate psychological and feminist dilemmas in a way which forces them to our notice.

Even the most explicitly political contributions to associative feminist psychology exert their influence through particular rhetorical structures, and function as signifiers, not translators, of realities. Ladner's account of young black women does not use the anecdotal and case history material it has gathered as psychology generally does, to illustrate a general proposition about psychological subjects. Instead, it presents individual women's subjectivities synecdochally, as a crystallization of all the social and historical relations that impinge on them.[3] The stories of Kim's and Beth's respectively unprotected and overprotected childhoods, are, Ladner says, 'models' (1979: 220) of two ends of a polarity of ways in which these influences can be worked out. This synecdochal strategy does not let Ladner spell out the whole of the complex relationship between subjectivity and power relations. But it, and not simply her use of social and historical explanations, is what allows her

to question the limitations of behavioural scientific accounts of socialization.

A similar approach is apparent in Bryan *et al.*'s work. *Heart of the
Race* uses quotations, not as examples, but to indicate the historical and
social relations of which these individual voices form a part. The quotations function as partial explanations, like any other element of the text.
The text can even be read as a collection of quotations from a number
of women, including the authors; or as a chorus of contradictory, even
self-contradictory, voices. Such work gives an account of the subjective
significance of discourses of gender, 'race', and class, but it does not
claim to provide a general theory of them, or to offer completely con-
vincing reasons for any individual woman's subjectivity. The following
quotation, allowed to stand for itself, without further explication, expresses this uncertainty:

> They never encouraged you or asked you what you would like to do
> when you leave school. I had always been made to feel that because
> I was Black, I was stupid and not good enough for much. You got
> that impression from TV as well – that we were just maids, butlers,
> servants in fact. My Careers Officer tried to send me to a factory
> interview. It was the best they felt they could do for someone with
> no 'O' levels. But I didn't turn up for the interview. Although I wasn't
> qualified, I didn't want a factory job.
>
> (Bryan *et al.* 1985: 68)

Through the contradictoriness of feeling stupid and refusing to accept
this feeling, the quotation creates a picture of a complex subjectivity,
unconscious as well as conscious, socially, historically and individually
determined, difficult to understand, and resistant, as well as restricted.

There is another, more general, example of associative feminist
psychology's rhetorical productiveness: the metaphorical connections it
makes with other critical discourses. Feminism is not an autonomous
field. It shares notions of subjectivity, equality and liberation with other
forms of resistance, and is socially and historically allied with them.
Whenever it is called upon, it evokes these other resistances metaphoric-
ally. Associative feminist psychologies' rhetorical interventions are
especially likely to do this. Many readings of Gilligan's 'different voice'
hypothesis, for instance, extend it, to cover oppressed human groups
other than women. Arguelles's and Rich's (1984) description of the
history of lesbians' and gay men's lives in Cuba is proposed as a guide
to understanding lesbian and gay experience in other Third World

countries and communities. *Heart of the Race*'s wide-ranging historical account of black women's experiences in Britain has induced British feminists, including some working in psychology, to consider similar approaches to issues of 'race' in other areas. Such metaphorical extensions can skip over the specificity of gender and other social relations, and become too over-generalized to be useful. But they keep difficult issues from being forgotten in psychology. This is particularly important now, when psychologists are retrenching, and supporting only the most modest and 'realistic' of critical initiatives.[4]

The account I have given of associative feminist psychology bears some resemblance to descriptions of deconstruction, a form of textual analysis developed mainly in France and North America.[5] Deconstruction has influenced feminist studies widely but feminists are often critical of its male-identified 'phallogocentrism'.[6] Psychoanalysts have discussed it.[7] A few psychologists have drawn on it (e.g. Henriques *et al.* 1984); Parker (1989) and Parker and Shotter (1989) even present it as a model for critical social psychology. What I have called 'associative' feminist psychology also comes close to deconstruction in some ways, while giving it a specifically psychological form.

Deconstruction involves considering the boundaries and limitations of a text, and relating what seems to be outside it, to what is inside. Like associative feminist psychologies, deconstruction sees the individual subject as fragmented, irrational, but persistent. Again, like associative feminist psychologies, it adopts a structuralist understanding of significations, though it does this in a much more systematic and reflexive way. It, too, works with textual ambiguities, and comments rhetorically on their rhetorics, though it is much more self-conscious about this project than associative feminist psychologies are. And deconstruction, too, manages, not simply to substitute subordinate for dominant meanings, or to suspend meaning between the two, but to analyse the residues of signification which are left outside polarized meanings, and in this way to shift debate to a new area and start again. Deconstructionists like Derrida also argue that 'writing' can be in any medium: there is nothing outside the text. And so, like associative feminist psychologies, deconstruction can address any manifestation of signifactory structure.

It is often claimed (e.g. Graff 1979, Said 1984) that deconstruction prolongs to infinity its analyses of textual structures, and cannot address social or historical change. The opposite criticism is directed at political versions of deconstruction (e.g. Ryan 1982, Spivak 1987). They are accused of reducing signifiers to indices of social relations. On the few occasions when psychologists invoke deconstruction, they tend to take this latter course, using it as a way to relate language to social relations, or to explain psychological discourses through uncovering the traces of their histories. They stress deconstruction's affinities with criticism, and play down its commentary function. But some writers whose work is called deconstructive suggest that deconstruction can avoid reducing the text's meanings to social or historical relations, or restricting their significance to a matter of textual play. They argue that, by focusing on particular cracks in the structure of a text's meaning, deconstruction can generate small discursive changes (Derrida 1981, Norris 1987, Spivak 1987). Derrida calls deconstruction of this kind, affirmative deconstruction. Deconstruction is frequently used in this way, against dominant discourses of gender and 'race', especially in literary theory, where it is most established.[8] Derrida's own persistent dissection of textual expressions of femininity and masculinity has altered the terms of literary critical debates about gender (e.g. Derrida 1978).

Deconstructive affirmations, like associative feminist psychologies, do not formulate complete alternatives to dominant discourses. Their realization of the complex relationships between language and discourse forces them to produce uncertainties, rather than final, truthful interpretations. In an attempt to avoid some of the totalizations which can compromise his work, Derrida refuses to declare it pro- or anti-feminist. And so, again like associative feminist psychologies, deconstruction preserves the status of a commentary, rather than of a more recuperable critique.

Most associative feminist psychologies omit one of deconstruction's most ubiquitous and productive concerns: its use of a psychoanalytic notion of the subject as structured by unconscious representations of sexual difference, to address the ambiguities of subjectivity. Deconstruction sees the unconscious in a wider context than most psychoanalysts or feminists do. Its textual analyses connect discourses of the unconscious to other discourses, and develop a kind of metapsychoanalysis, which presents the unconscious as the centre and simultaneously the ex-centre of western discourses. Derrida thinks that psychoanalysis can stimulate a reconsideration of powerful discourses of law, morality, politics, and psychiatry.[9] As the last chapter showed, psychoanalysis also has a lot to offer feminist psychologies. But when these psychologies address it, they often become paralysed by it. Deconstruction's broader psychoanalytic commitment is something associative feminist psychologies could usefully adopt.

Associative feminist psychology seems to go beyond deconstructive affirmation in some ways. It has a more direct relation to questions of power, and is less interested in the fine structure of language, than most deconstructive initiatives are. In this, it comes nearer to Said's (1984) notion of criticism as a kind of affiliation. Said describes twentieth-century western critics' concern with the loss or failure of an intellectual life based on filiation: known, stable, even biological relations to particular social worlds. He suggests that critics' attempts to recapitulate the communities inherent in such relations by affiliating to social institutions, often recapitulate the authoritarian aspects of filiation. But they need not do so. Affiliative criticism 'sometimes makes its own forms' (Said 1984: 24). These forms resemble the associations which I have described operating in feminist psychology. They too question discursive boundaries, and establish connections outside them. But the filiation metaphor is not ideal for feminist psychology. It would intensify the already strong individualism of psychology, and the problems which concepts of the family provoke within both psychology and feminism. The less specific 'association' metaphor works better. The term also suits the extreme insularity of psychology. The discipline omits, not just close, filiative ties, but the whole of social relations. Most psychology does not even see these as lost; it deliberately excludes or tries to avoid them. The cautious characterization of feminist psychology's aims as 'associative' fits with this extreme asociality.

Associative initiatives develop the kinds of specific, detailed yet open account of subjectivity and power relations that feminist psychology needs. They help it to break away from traditional restrictions on psychological field, method, and theory; to look at how gender, 'race', and class interests affect discourses of the subject; and still to have a place within psychology. But even associative feminist psychologies only generate partial, temporary changes.

Psychology's carefully defended structures depend heavily on dominant discourses of gender. It is important for feminists to challenge this dependency, both because issues of subjectivity are central for feminism, and because the study of gender is increasingly significant in psychology. But it is difficult to produce a feminist psychology that is not ultimately reducible to conventional psychology's primary concept of the individual subject. Faced with psychology's intransigence, today's definitive feminist alternative becomes idealized, co-opted, or marginalized tomorrow. Such limitations are unavoidable. A flexible, piecemeal feminist psychology, always generating new strategies to keep the discourse under scrutiny, is the most we can hope for. This book has described some strategies of this kind, and the problems they encounter. To go on producing such initiatives, feminist psychology needs, as Unger says in her paper 'Through the looking glass: no wonderland yet', to be wary of truth, and not search for final answers. 'The questions will not go away' (1983: 28). Unger's title invokes realms characterized by uncertainty, particularly uncertainty in signification. Feminist psychology should not step back from these territories. It will need to live within them for a long time.

Notes

Introduction

1 The concept of discourse used in the book is drawn from Foucault's later work (e.g. Foucault 1979).
2 This book refers throughout to discourses of gender, not discourses of sex and gender. This is not a denial of biological differences, but a way of avoiding conventional psychology's simplifying dichotomy between 'sex' and 'gender'.

Chapter 1   Counting women in

1 Ball and Bourner (1984), Over (1984), Smith and Casbolt (1984), and Kornbrot (1987) provide insights on women's position within British psychology.
2 Unger (1979), Russo (1982), Walsh (1985), the APA Committee on Employment and Human Resources (1986), Basow (1986), and Bronstein *et al*. (1986), survey different aspects of women's participation in US psychology.
3 Unger (1979), Walsh (1985), and Basow (1986) describe feminist organizations in US psychology. Wilkinson (1988) gives an account of the developments in the BPS.
4 This happens especially often in psychoanalysis, since a very strong form of lineage is set up by training analyses. Early female analysts analysed by Freud, like Deutsch, are good examples (Roazen 1985).
5 The problems which arise in feminist psychology from such a general characterization of discursive 'power' are considered in Chapter 6.
6 I shall concentrate on the categories which seem to have most impact on psychological discourses of gender, although it could be argued that the expectations associated with others, like marriage (Furumoto and Scarsborough 1986), pregnancy (Taylor and Langer quoted in Unger 1979), and disability, may also interact with gender in important ways.
7 Brown (1973) encapsulates this outrage. Billig (1982) provides later, more subtle analyses of psychology's relationship to class-structured ideologies.

8 This book refers predominantly to black psychologists and subjects when describing discriminations on the grounds of 'race', not to deny differences between these psychologists and subjects, or other, political difficulties with the reference, but because western psychology and its critics see 'race' discriminations as exercised mainly against groups defined as black. The book writes 'race' in inverted commas throughout to mark the problematic way the word is generally used in psychology, as a sign of a discrete biological or cultural group.

9 The APA Committee on Employment and Human Resources (1986) reviews black and ethnic minority participation in US psychology. The *Chronicle of Higher Education* documented a range of evidence of black and ethnic minority students' and professors' decreasing representation throughout academia, throughout 1987.

10 Such criticisms include Guthrie (1976), Jones (1980), McAdoo (1981), Lawrence (1983), Henriques (1984), Billig (1985), Brown *et al.* (1985), Bryan *et al.* (1985), and Condor (1986a). The BPS Standing Committee on Equal Opportunities is also now monitoring alleged 'psychologists'' reports on 'race' differences for racism (Ussher 1987).

11 Examples of such work include Wilson (1978), Carby (1983), Parmar (1983), Bryan *et al.* (1985), and Grewal *et al.* (1988), and, in the US, Rodgers Rose (1980), Moraga and Anzaldúa (1981), Hooks (1982), Smith (1983) and Walker (1984).

12 Journals which provide a forum for these psychologists include the *Journal of Black Psychology* and the *Journal of Black Studies*.

13 Publications which support such work include the *Journal of Homosexuality, Signs*, and *Heresies*.

Chapter 2   A balanced subject

1 As Canguilhem says,

> The characteristic unity of the concept of a science has traditionally been taken as deriving from the object of that science . . . contrary to appearances, it is in terms more of its object than of its method that a discipline is called psychology.
>
> (1980: 38)

2 Maccoby and Jacklin (1974), Lloyd and Archer (1976), Hartnett *et al.* (1979), Unger (1979), Nicholson (1984), and Archer and Lloyd (1985) provide general accounts of sex differences which adopt a broadly egalitarian perspective and are influenced by or explicitly committed to feminism. Important specific reviews of sex differences include Deaux (1976) on attributions; Frodi *et al.* (1977), Maccoby and Jacklin (1980), Tieger (1980), and Eagly and Steffen (1986) on aggression; Henley (1977) on non-verbal communication; Eagly (1978) on influenceability; Walker (1984, 1986) and Baumrind (1986) on moral reasoning; Caplan *et al.* (1985) on spatial abilities; and Tittle (1986) on mathematical abilities.

3 Berg *et al.* (1981) restrict this term to low internal and high external attributions of success. High internal and low external attributions of failure are termed self-derogation.

4 Tieger (1980) makes this point about aggression, Burnett (1986), Caplan *et al.* (1986) and Halpern (1986) about spatial abilities.

5 Examples are Auerbach *et al.* (1985) in *Feminist Studies*; Greeno and Maccoby (1986), Kerber (1986), Luria (1986) and Stack (1986) in *Signs*; and *New Ideas in Psychology* 1987 5(2).

6 Useful summaries and collections of work on the psychology of women include Sherman (1971), Bardwick (1971a,b, 1972), Fransella and Frost (1977), Unger (1979), Williams (1979, 1985), Cox (1981), and Hyde (1985), Wilkinson (1986a) includes examples of such work in the specific area of social psychology. Valuable examples of feminist revisions of psychological work on mother-child relations are the work of McAdoo (1981), Mayall and Petrie (1983), Dunn (1984), McAdoo and McAdoo (1985), New and David (1985), Urwin (1985), and Tizard (1987).

7 Archer quotes mathematical ability and childrearing practices; Tizard and Hughes (1984) back up the latter suggestion.

8 McRobbie and McCabe (1981), McRobbie and Nava (1984), and Sharpe (1984, 1987) provide a range of feminist perspectives on young women's experiences. Hemmings (1985) begins to document the lives of older women.

9 Stoller's work is an exception, including a number of studies of lesbians and one long case history (e.g. 1974).

10 Watters (1986) reviews the liberalization in psychology's approach to homosexuality over the past decade. Cass (1984), Duffy and Risbult (1985–6), Harris and Turner (1985–6) and Sophie (1985–6) are examples of comparison-oriented accounts. Work dealing more specifically with lesbian subjectivity includes that of Ponse (1978), Ettore (1980), Bristow and Pearn (1984), and Darty and Potter (1984). Some accounts distance themselves from a straightforwardly affirmative approach, such as Krieger (1986), Sandoval (1984), Arguelles and Rich (1984), Dominy (1986), and Kitzinger (1987).

11 The psychology of black women is explored outside the white-dominated feminist psychology of women but within a relatively orthodox psychological approach within work like that of McAdoo (1981), Martinez (1984), McAdoo and McAdoo (1985), and the *Journal of Black Psychology*. More radical approaches to psychology feature occasionally in the *Journal of Black Studies*, and in sociological studies like that of Ladner (1979) and Stack (1975). The books mentioned in note 1 for Chapter 1 address important aspects of black women's subjectivities.

Chapter 3 Designs for equality

1 Maslow accepts this about his work (Maslow and Chiang 1977).

2 Marcus (1987) discusses the assumptions about identity which characterize popular autobiographical feminist methods.

3 This is much less true of feminist therapists.

4 The special section on Feminist Research in *Psychology of Women Quarterly*

5(4), Summer 1981, exemplifies this approach.

5 Androgyny in women is also related to extraversion, low alcoholism, creativity, intimate relations, and lower sexual inhibitions (Kaplan and Sedney 1980), and to sense of competence, stress invulnerability, lack of stress symptoms, and comfortableness with displaying feminine and masculine behaviours (Heilbrun 1984). Androgynous men, on the other hand, differ little from masculine, sex-typed men, except that they report more drinking problems, and score lower on feelings of control over their behaviour, and on extraversion, political awareness, and creativity (Kaplan and Sedney 1980).

6 Among the feminist psychologists interested in methodological change who maintain scientificity as their aim are Brannon (1981), Parlee (1981), and Unger (1982).

7 Gossett (1981), Wong (1981), and Johnson (1983) give vivid accounts of the power of such expressive possibilities.

Chapter 4   Theory for all

1 Parlee (1979), Fine (1985), Henley (1985), and Lott (1985) all give good accounts of feminist psychological theory in general, and this tendency in particular.

2 Riley (1983) provides a detailed and subtle description of this relationship.

3 Feminist accounts of gender bias in biology include Sayers (1982), Birke (1986), and Harding (1986).

4 Sociobiologists argue that in the case of male parenting among water-living species, the greater stability of females' genetic material may allow them to leave the eggs and force males to care for the fertilized embryos (Dawkins 1978: 167–9). But in some invertebrate species, too, females, males, or occasionally both, protect eggs and young, depending on the severity of the habitat (Wyatt 1987). Dawkins's work on sex draws heavily on Trivers (1972). Maynard Smith's (1978) consideration of sex differences in an evolutionary perspective is more cautious, and involves less generalizing from animals to humans.

5 Montagu (1980) gives a more specific critique of sociobiology. Coward (1984) describes relationships between popular discourses of biology and gender. Hirst and Wooley (1982) provide a good assessment of the difficulties of biological explanations of psychological and social characteristics, including those associated with gender.

6 Morgan and Ayim (1984) have criticized the reproductive and heterosexist orientation of the schemata Bem puts forward. Bem's reply supplements her sex difference schema with the clitoris, but still preserves a kind of reproductive order: 'penis and testicles, vagina and clitoris' (1984: 198). Bem emphasizes that she is interested in anatomical and reproductive schemata, which deal with sex differences only where they make a biological difference. Her mention of the clitoris seems unnecessary in this framework. And why stop with the vagina? What about the breasts, uterus and Fallopian tubes? Particular heterosexuality schemata seem still to be operating.

7 Condor (1986a, b) has produced useful descriptions of how this psychologized justification of the status quo operates in the psychology of 'race' and gender stereotypes.
8 Sherif (1977), Clifford and Frosh (1982), Unger (1983), Henley (1985), Wittig (1985), and Handy (1987) provide good examples.

Chapter 5   Woman-centred psychology

1 Segal (1987) and Coote and Campbell (1987) give good accounts of this controversy.
2 Cox (1981) reviews the psychology of women from this perspective.
3 Auerbach *et al.* (1985), Henley (1985), Kerber (1986), and Luria (1986) all voice concern about Gilligan's feminine essentialism or the possibility of reading her work in this way.

Chapter 6   The unconscious and discourse

1 Freud was not the first to formulate a concept of the unconscious, as Whyte (1967) makes clear. However, he was the first to put it in a psychological framework.
2 Rowbotham *et al.*'s (1979) attempts at this continue a long tradition, beginning with Freud's psychohistories of institutions and cultures, and proceeding less reductively in the work of Reich, Marcuse, and Adorno.
3 Althusser (1972) and Metz (1982) are good examples. In France, some adopted psychoanalysis almost as an alternative to politics after 1968 (Turkle 1979, Moi 1987), a position it could be argued it has in Britain today (Frosh 1987).
4 Gallop (1982), Kaplan herself (1986), and Felman (1987) provide good examples in literary studies; Kuhn and Wolpe (1982), Doane (1983), and De Lauretis (1984) in film studies, Coward (1984) in cultural studies, and Mitchell (1974), and *m/f* in a more general political arena.
5 Instances include the work of Mitchell (1974), Coward and Ellis (1977), and the journals *Ideology and Consciousness* and *m/f*.
6 Woman-centred theorists like Daly (1979) and Spender (1980) have been especially interested in this work. Cameron (1985) gives a critical account of this work and considers other structuralist and semiotic perspectives.
7 Lakoff (1975) deals with language and gender from a psychological perspective. Pleck (1975) and Deaux (1976) are examples of psychologists who take language seriously within their accounts of gender.
8 Many feminists deny that Lacanian psychoanalysis has any relevance to their work (e.g. Wilson 1981). Others recognize its limitations, but remain interested in it (e.g. Mitchell 1974, Coward 1978, Sayers 1986).
9 Adlam and Salfield (1978) give a good account of the difficulties and contradictions in Coward and Ellis's work.
10 This has happened more generally in psychology, in, for example, Rose's

(1985) mapping out of ideas and practices of psychological regulations and control, and Parker's (1989) analysis of the discursive histories of social psychology. The approach has also been used widely and eclectically to analyse different articulations of power in such areas as education, popular culture, and social welfare (e.g. Donzelot 1980). In particular the universal potential for sexuality which forms an unquestioned basis even of feminist Lacanianism is made into a discursive matter (e.g. Heath 1982).

Chapter 7 Forming associations

1 The structures of psychological and non-psychological narratives are explored in Squire (1989a).
2 The disruption of psychology by analyses which bypass the discipline's conventional boundaries has happened in other areas of black psychology, for instance in Afrocentric psychology (Nobles 1980, Baldwin 1985), and in Stack's (1975) research on feelings of kinship among black American return migrants to the south.
3 Schor (1981) recommends synecdoche as a strategy for feminist theory in general. She bases this argument on dominant discourses' physicalization of femininity. She proposes that feminists need to use signifiers of the part of the body whose existence dominant discourses of femininity deny, the clitoris, to stand for all aspects of their excluded experience.
4 Squire (1989b) examines the wider critical effects of feminist psychology among psychology students and teachers.
5 Deconstruction was originally a philosophical initiative (e.g. Derrida 1976, 1977, 1979), but it has extensive influence in literary and cultural studies, and has provoked strong opposition in these fields (e.g. De Man 1979, Graff 1979, Hartman 1981, Culler 1983, *Screen* 28 (1) Winter 1987). It is a term applied to and claimed by very variable forms of work. My account focuses mainly on Derrida's work, because of its historical span, its encompassing of most of deconstruction's contradictions and debates in a complex way, its development and changes, and the frequency with which it is referred to by other deconstructive work.
6 Examples include Johnson (1977, 1987) and Spivak (1981, 1987).
7 Psychoanalysts have, however, seen deconstruction as primarily of philosophical relevance, or at best as a kind of inferior psychoanalysis for non-analysts (e.g. Derrida 1980: 525–49, Major 1982).
8 Gates (ed.) (1986), especially Bhabha, Pratt, Derrida, and Spivak, and Spivak (1987) give interesting indications of where such work may lead.
9 But Derrida is pessimistic about this actually happening, in psychoanalysis or outside it.

References

Adams, P. (1983) 'Mothering', *m/f* 8: 41-52.

Adlam, D. and Salfield, A. (1978) 'A matter of language', *Ideology and Consciousness* 3: 95-111.

Aitkenhead, M. (1987) 'Psychology of women section', *British Psychological Society Bulletin* 40: 299.

Alladin, W. (1988) Introduction to Skinner's 'Whatever happened to psychology as the science of behavior?', *Counselling Psychology Quarterly* 1: 111-12.

Althusser, L. (1972) *Lenin and Philosophy*, London: Verso.

American Psychological Association Committee on Employment and Human Resources (1986) 'The changing face of American psychology', *American Psychologist* 41: 1311-27.

Anderson, C. and Henderson, D. (1985) 'Working with lesbian alcoholics', *Social Work* November-December 30: 518-25.

Archer, J. (1987) 'Beyond sex differences', *Bulletin of the British Psychological Society* 40: 88-90.

Archer, J. and Lloyd, B. (1985) *Sex and Gender*, Cambridge: Cambridge University Press.

Ardill, S. and O'Sullivan, S. (1986) 'Upsetting an applecart', *Feminist Review* 23: 31-57.

Arguelles, L. and Rich, R. (1984) 'Homosexuality, homophobia and revolution', *Signs* 9: 683-99.

Arpad, S. (1986) 'Burnout', *Women's Studies International Forum* 9: 207-13.

Auerbach, J., Blum, L., Smith, V., and Williams, C. (1985) 'Commentary on Gilligan's "In a different voice"', *Feminist Studies* 11: 149-62.

Baldwin, J. (1985) 'African (Black) psychology: issues and synthesis', *Journal of Black Studies* 16: 235-49.

Ball, B., and Bourner, T. (1984) 'The employment of psychology graduates', *Bulletin of the British Psychological Society* 37: 39-40.

Bardwick, J. (1971a) *The Psychology of Women*, New York: Harper & Row.

—— (1971b) *On the Psychology of Women: A Survey of Empirical Studies*, Springfield, Mass.: Charles Thomas.

—— (ed.) (1972) *Readings in the Psychology of Women*, New York: Harper & Row.

Barnett, R. and Baruch, G. (1985) 'Women in the middle years', in J. Williams (ed.) *Psychology of Women: Selected Readings*, New York: Norton.

Barrett, C. (1985) 'Intimacy in widowhood', in J. Williams (ed.) *Psychology of Women: Selected Readings*, New York: Norton.

Barrett, M. (1987) 'The concept of "Difference"', *Feminist Review* 26: 29–42.

Basow, S. (1986) 'The psychology of women: a view from the States', *Equal Opportunities International* 5 (3/4): 3–7.

Baumrind, D. (1982) 'Are androgynous individuals more effective persons and parents?', *Child Development* 53: 44–75.

—— (1986) 'Sex differences in the development of moral reasoning: response to Walker's (1984) conclusion that there are none', *Child Development* 55: 511–21.

Beattie, G. (1987) *Making It*, London: Weidenfeld & Nicholson.

Beckett, H. (1986) 'Cognitive developmental theory in the study of adolescent identity development', in S. Wilkinson (ed.) *Feminist Social Psychology*, Milton Keynes: Open University Press.

Bell, G. and Schaffer, K. (1984) 'The effects of androgyny on attributions of causality for success and failure', *Sex Roles* 11: 1045–55.

Beloff, H. (1980) 'Are models of man models of women?', in Chapman and Jones (eds) *Models of Man*, Leicester: British Psychological Society.

Bem, S. (1974) 'The measurement of psychological androgyny', *Journal of Consulting and Clinical Psychology* 42: 155–62.

—— (1977) 'On the utility of alternative procedures for assessing psychological androgyny', *Journal of Consulting and Clinical Psychology* 45: 196–205.

—— (1979a) 'Theory and measurement of androgyny: a reply to the Pedhazur-Tetenbaum and Locksley-Colten critiques', *Journal of Personality and Social Psychology* 37: 1047–54.

—— (1979b) 'Beyond androgyny: some presumptuous prescriptions for a liberated sexual identity', in J. Sherman and F. Denmark (eds) *The Future of Women: Issues in Psychology*, New York: Psychological Dimensions.

—— (1983) 'Gender schema theory and its implications for child development: raising gender-aschematic children in a gender-schematic society', *Signs* 8: 598–616.

—— (1984) 'Reply to Morgan and Ayim', *Signs* 10: 197–9.

Berg, J., Stephan, W. and Dodson, M. (1981) 'Attributional modesty in women', *Psychology of Women Quarterly* 5: 711–27.

Bhabha, H. (1986) 'Signs taken for wonders', in H. Gates (ed.) *Race, Writing and Difference*, Oxford: Oxford University Press.

Billig, M. (1982) *Ideology and Social Psychology*, Oxford: Blackwell.

—— (1985) 'Prejudice, categorisation, and particularisation: from a perceptual to a rhetorical account', *European Journal of Social Psychology* 15: 79–105.

Birke, L. (1986) *Women, Feminism and Biology*, London: Wheatsheaf.

Borrill, J. and Reid, B. (1986) 'Are British psychologists interested in sex differences?', *Bulletin of the British Psychology Society* 39: 286–8.

Brannon, R. (1981) 'Current methodological issues in pencil and paper measuring instruments', *Psychology of Women Quarterly* 5: 618–27.

Bristow, A. and Pearn, P. (1984) 'Comment on Krieger's "Identity and lesbian community: recent social science literature''', *Signs* 9: 729–32.

Bronstein, P., Black, L., Pfennig, J. and White, A. (1986) 'Getting academic jobs: are women equally qualified and equally successful?', *American Psychologist* 41: 318–22.

Brown, A., Goodwin, B., Hall, B. and Jackson-Lowman, H. (1985) 'A review of psychology of women textbooks: focus on the Afro-American woman', *Psychology of Women Quarterly* 9: 29–38.

Brown, P. (ed.) (1973) *Radical Psychology*, New York: Harper Colophon.

Bryan, B., Dadzie, S. and Scafe, S. (1985) *The Heart of the Race*, London: Virago.

Burnett, S. (1986) 'Sex-related differences in spatial ability: are they trivial?', *American Psychologist* 41: 1012–13.

Burns, J. and de Jong, M. (1986) 'Introduction', *Equal Opportunities International* 5 (3/4): 1–2.

Butler, N. and Golding, J. (1986) *From Birth to Five*, London: Pergamon.

Califia, P. (1980) 'The sexual fringe', *ZG* 2.

Cameron, D. (1985) *Feminism and Linguistic Theory*, London: Macmillan.

Campbell, B. (1987) *The Iron Ladies*, London: Virago.

Canguilhem, G. (1980) 'What is psychology?', *Ideology and Consciousness* 7: 37–50.

Caplan, P. (1981) *Barriers Between Women*, Lancaster: MTP Press Ltd.

Caplan, P., MacPherson, G. and Tobin, P. (1985) 'Do sex-related differences in spatial ability exist? A multilevel critique with new data', *American Psychologist* 40: 786–99.

—— (1986) 'The magnified molehill and the misplaced focus: sex related differences in spatial ability revisited', *American Psychologist* 41: 1016–18.

Carby, H. (1983) 'White woman listen! Black feminism and the boundaries of sisterhood', in Centre for Contemporary Cultural Studies (ed.) *The Empire Strikes Back*, London: Hutchinson.

Cass, V. (1984) 'Homosexual identity formation: testing a theoretical model', *Journal of Sex Research* 20: 143–67.

Chasseguet-Smirgel, J. (1985) *The Ego Ideal*, London: Free Association.

Chernin, K. (1986) *The Hungry Self*, London: Virago.

Chesler, P. (1974) *Women and Madness*, London: Allen Lane.

Chodorow, N. (1978) *The Reproduction of Mothering*, Los Angeles: University of California Press.

Clifford, P. and Frosh, S. (1982) 'Towards a non-essentialist psychology: a linguistic framework', *Bulletin of the British Psychological Society* 35: 267–70.

Condor. S. (1986a) 'The eye of the beholder and the myopia of the researcher: social psychological approaches to ''stereotypes'' and stereotyping', British Psychological Society Social Psychological Section conference: Cambridge University.

—— (1986b) 'Sex role beliefs and ''traditional'' psychology', in S. Wilkinson (ed.) *Feminist Social Psychology*, Milton Keynes: Open University Press.

Condry, J. and Dyer, S. (1976) 'Fear of success: attribution of cause to the victim', *Journal of Social Issues* 32: 62–83.

Coote, A. and Campbell, B.(1987) *Sweet Freedom*, Oxford: Blackwell.

Cousins, M. and Hussain, A. (1984) *Michel Foucault*, London: Macmillan.

Coward, R. (1983) *Patriarchal Precedents*, London: Routledge & Kegan Paul.

—— (1984) *Female Desire*, London: Paladin.

Coward, R. and Ellis, J. (1977) *Language and Materialism*, London: Routledge & Kegan Paul.

Cox. S. (ed.) (1981) *Female Psychology*, Chicago: Science Research Associates.

Culler, J. (1983) *On Deconstruction*, London: Routledge & Kegan Paul.

Cutmore-Smith, J. (1986) 'Exploring the dark: women, power and work', *Equal Opportunities International* 5 (3/4): 32–5.

Daly, M. (1979) *Gyn/Ecology*, London: Women's Press.

Dancey, C. (1987) 'Is a distinction between primary and secondary lesbianism warranted?', Women in Psychology Conference: Brunel University.

Darty, T. and Potter, S. (eds) (1984) *Woman-Identified Women*, Palo Alto, California: Mayfield.

Dawkins, R. (1978) *The Selfish Gene*, London: Granada.

—— (1982) *The Extended Phenotype*, Oxford: Oxford University Press.

—— (1986) *The Blind Watchmaker*, London: Longman.

Deaux, K. (1976) 'Sex: a perspective on the attribution process', in J. Harvey, W. Ickes and R. Kidd (eds) *New Directions in Attribution Research*, Hillsdale, New Jersey: Erlbaum.

De Lauretis, T. (1984) *Alice Doesn't*, London: Macmillan.

De Man, P. (1979) *Allegories of Reading*, New Haven: Yale University Press.

Derrida, J. (1976) *Of Grammatology*, Baltimore and London: Johns Hopkins University Press.

—— (1977), *Edmund Husserl's 'The Origins of Geometry'*, Nebraska: University of Nebraska Press.

—— (1978) *Spurs*, Chicago: University of Chicago Press.

—— (1979) *Writing And Difference*, London: Routledge & Kegan Paul.

—— (1980) *La Carte Postale*, Paris: Flammarion.

—— (1981) *Positions*, Chicago: University of Chicago Press.

—— (1985) 'Racism's last word', *Critical Inquiry* 12: 291–9.

Diamond, N. (1985) 'Thin is the feminist issue', *Feminist Review* 19: 45–65.

Dickson, A. (1982) *A Woman In Your Own Right*, London: Quartet.

Dinnerstein, D. (1976) *The Mermaid and the Minotaur*, New York: Harper & Row.

Doane, M. (ed.) (1983) *Re-visions*, New York: University Publications of America.

Dominy, M. (1986) 'Lesbian-feminist gender conceptions: separatism in Christchurch, New Zealand', *Signs* 11: 274–89.

Donzelot, J. (1980) *The Policing of Families*, London: Hutchinson Education.

Douglas, A. (1986) 'Take the toys from the boys', *Equal Opportunities International* 5 (3/4): 28–31.

Duffy, S. and Risbult, C. (1985–6) 'Satisfaction and commitment in homosexual and heterosexual relationships', *Journal of Homosexuality* 12 (2): 1–23.

Dunn, J. (1984) *Sisters and Brothers*, London: Fontana.

Duveen, G. and Lloyd, B. (1986) 'The significance of social identities', *British Journal of Social Psychology* 25: 219–50.

Dworkin, A. (1981) *Pornography*, London: Women's Press.

Eagly, A. (1978) 'Sex differences in influenceability', *Psychological Bulletin* 85: 86–116.

Eagly, A. and Steffen, V. (1986) 'Gender and aggressive behavior', *Psychological Bulletin* 100: 309–30.

Eichenbaum, S. and Orbach, S. (1982) *Outside In, Inside Out*, Harmondsworth: Penguin

Ernst, S. and Goodison, L. (1981) *In Our Own Hands*, London: Routledge & Kegan Paul.

Ettore, E. (1980) *Lesbians, Women and Society*, London: Routledge & Kegan Paul.

Eysenck, H. (1973) *The Experimental Study of Freudian Theories*, London: Methuen

Farrell, B. (1981) *The Standing of Psychoanalysis*, Oxford: Oxford University Press.

Felman, S. (1987) *Jacques Lacan and the Adventure of Insight*, Cambridge, Mass.: Harvard University Press.

Figes, E. (1972) *Patriarchal Attitudes*, London: Panther.

Fine, M. (1985) 'Reflections on feminist psychology of women: paradoxes and perspectives', *Psychology of Women Quarterly* 9: 167–83.

Firestone, S. (1971) *The Dialectic Of Sex*, London: Cape.

Flanagan, O. (1982) 'Virtue, sex and gender', *Ethics* 92: 499–512.

Foucault, M. (1979) *The History of Sexuality*, London: Allen Lane.

—— (1982) 'The subject and power', *Critical Inquiry* 8: 777–95.

Fransella, F. and Frost, K. (1977) *On Being a Woman*, London: Tavistock.

Freud, S. (1905) 'Three essays on sexuality', in *Standard Edition* vol. VII, London: Hogarth.

—— (1920) 'Psychogenesis of a case of homosexuality in a woman', in *Standard Edition* vol. XVIII, London: Hogarth.

—— (1933) 'New introductory lectures on psycho-analysis', in *Standard Edition* vol. XXII, London: Hogarth.

Friedan, B. (1965) *The Feminine Mystique*, Harmondsworth: Penguin.

Frodi, A., Macaulay, J. and Thome, P. (1977) 'Are women always less aggressive than men?', *Psychology Bulletin* 84: 634–60.

Frosh, S. (1987) *Politics of Psychoanalysis*, London: Macmillan Education.

Furnell, P. (1986) 'Lesbian and gay psychology', *Bulletin of the British Psychological Society* 39: 41–7.

Furumoto, L. and Scarsborough, E. (1986) 'Placing women in the history of psychology', *American Psychologist* 42: 35–42.

Gallop, J. (1982) *Feminism and Psychoanalysis*, London: Macmillan.

Gama, F. (1985) 'Achievement motivation of women: effects of achievement and affiliation arousal', *Psychology of Women Quarterly* 9: 89–103.

Gardiner, J. (1987) 'Self psychology as feminist theory', *Signs* 12: 761–80.

Gates, H. (ed.) (1986) *'Race', Writing and Difference*, Oxford: Oxford University Press.

Gessler, S. and Tyerman, C. (1982) 'Sex differences in clinical psychology recruitment', *Bulletin of the British Psychological Society* 35: 35.

Gilligan, C. (1982) *In A Different Voice*, Cambridge, Mass.: Harvard University Press.

—— (1986) 'Reply', *Signs* 11: 324–33.

Gossett, H. (1981) 'Who told you anybody wants to hear from you? You ain't nothing but a black woman!' in C. Moraga and G. Anzaldúa (eds) *This Bridge Called My Back*, Watertown, Mass.: Persephone Press.

Grady, K. (1981) 'Sex bias in research design', *Psychology of Women Quarterly* 5: 628–36.

Graff, G. (1979) *Literature Against Itself*, Chicago: University of Chicago Press.

Greeno, C. and Maccoby, E. (1986) 'How different is the "different voice"?', *Signs* 11: 310–16.

Greer, G. (1971) *The Female Eunuch*, London: Paladin.

Grewal, S., Kay, J., Landor, L., Lewis, G. and Parmar, P. (1988) *Charting the Journey*, London: Sheba.

Griffen, S. (1979) 'A cross-cultural investigation of behavioral changes at menopause', in J. Williams (ed.) *Psychology of Women: Selected Readings*, New York: Norton.

Griffin, C. (1986) 'Qualitative methods and female experience: young women from school to the job market', in S. Wilkinson (ed.) *Feminist Social Psychology*, Milton Keynes: Open University Press.

Griffin, S. (1982) *Made From This Earth*, London: Women's Press.

Guthrie, R. (1976) *Even the Rat was White*, New York: Harper & Row.

Habermas, J. (1978) *Knowledge and Human Interests*, London: Heinemann.

Halpern, D. (1986) 'A different answer to the question: do sex-related differences in spatial abilities exist?', *American Psychologist* 41: 1014–15.

Handy, J. (1987) 'Psychology and social context', *Bulletin of the British Psychological Society* 40: 161–7.

Hanfmann, E.(1983) 'Autobiographical sketch', in A. O'Connell and N. Russo (eds) *Models of Achievement: Reflections of Eminent Women in Psychology*, New York: Columbia University Press.

Harari, H. and Peters, J. (1987) 'The fragmentation of psychology: are APA Divisions symptomatic?', *American Psychologist* 42: 822–4.

Harding, S. (1986) *The Science Question in Feminism*, Milton Keynes: Open University Press.

Hardyment, C. (1983) *Dream Babies*, London: Cape.

Harré, R. and Secord, P. (1972) *The Explanation of Social Behaviour*, Oxford: Blackwell.

Harris, M. and Turner, P. (1985–6) 'Gay and lesbian parents', *Journal of Homosexuality* 12 (2): 101–13.

Hartman, G. (1981) *Saving the Text*, Baltimore: Johns Hopkins University Press.

Hartnett, O., Boden, G. and Fuller, M. (1979) *Sex-Role Stereotyping*, London: Tavistock.

Hartnett, O. and Shimmen, S. (1987) 'On keeping psychology to ourselves, *Bulletin of the British Psychological Society* 40: 321–3.

Haug, F. (1987) 'Daydreams', *New Left Review* 167: 51–66.

Heath, S. (1982) *The Sexual Fix*, London: Macmillan.

Heilbrun, A. (1984) 'Androgyny as type and androgyny as behaviour: implications for gender schema in men and women', *Sex Roles* 14: 123–39.

Heilbrun, C. (1982) *Towards a Recognition of Androgyny*, New York: Norton.

Hemmings, S. (1985) *A Wealth of Experience*, London: Pandora.

Henlé, M. (1983) 'Autobiographical sketch', in A. O'Connell and N. Russo (eds) *Models of Achievement: Reflections of Eminent Women in Psychology*, New York: Columbia University Press.

Henley, N. (1977) *Body Politics*, New York: Simon & Schuster.

—— (1985) 'Psychology and gender', *Signs* 11: 101–19.

Henriques, J. (1984) 'Social psychology and the politics of racism', in J. Henriques *et al.* (eds) *Changing the Subject*, London: Methuen.

Henriques, J., Hollway, W., Urwin, C., Venn, C. and Walkerdine, V. (eds) (1984) *Changing the Subject*, London: Methuen.

Herriot, P. (1987) 'On keeping psychology to ourselves', *Bulletin of the British Psychological Society* 40: 430.

Hirst, P. and Wooley, P. (1982) *Social Relations and Human Attributes*, London: Tavistock.

Hiscock, M. (1986) 'On sex differences in spatial abilities', *American Psychologist* 41: 101–2.

Hobson, D. (1981) 'Now that I'm married . . . ', in A. McRobbie and T. McCabe (eds) *Feminism For Girls*, London: Routledge & Kegan Paul.

Hobson, S. (1970) 'Women and television', in R. Morgan (ed.) *Sisterhood is Powerful*, London: Vintage.

Hollway, W. (1984) 'Fitting work', in J. Henriques *et al.* (eds) *Changing the Subject*, London: Methuen.

Hooks, B. (1982) *Ain't I A Woman*, London: Pluto.

Horner, M. (1972) 'Towards an understanding of achievement-related conflicts in women', *Journal of Social Issues* 28 (2): 157–76.

Humphrey, M. and Haward, L. (1981) 'Sex differences in clinical psychology recruitment', *Bulletin of the British Psychological Society* 34: 413–14.

—— (1982) Letter, *Bulletin of the British Psychological Society* 35: 317.

Hussain, A. (1981) 'Review of History of Sexuality', *m/f* 5/6: 169–91.

Hutt, C. (1972) *Males and Females*, Harmondsworth: Penguin.

Hyde, J. (ed.) (1985) *Half The Human Experience*, Lexington, Mass.: Heath & Company

Irigaray, L. (1985) *Speculum: of the Other Woman*, Ithaca, New York: Cornell University Press.

Johnson, B. (1977) 'The frame of reference: Poe, Lacan, Derrida', *Yale French Studies* 55–6: 457–505.

—— (1987) *A World of Difference*, Baltimore: Johns Hopkins University Press.

Johnson, E. (1983) 'Reflections on black feminist therapy', in B. Smith (ed.) *Home Girls*, New York: Kitchen Table Press.

Jones, R. (ed.) (1980) *Black Psychology*, New York: Harper & Row.

Jones, W., Chernovetz, M. and Hannson, R. (1978) 'The psychology of androgyny: differential implications for males and females?', *Journal of Consulting and Clinical Psychology* 46: 298–313.

Kaplan, A. and Sedney, M. (1980) *Psychology and Sex Roles: An Androgynous Perspective*, Toronto: Little, Brown & Company.

Kaplan, C. (1986) *Sea Changes*, London: Verso.

Kerber, L. (1986) 'Some cautionary words for historians', *Signs* 11: 304–10.

Kimmel, M. (1988) *Changing Men*, New York: Sage.

Kippax, S., Crawford, J., Benton, P., Gault, U. and Noesjirwan, J. (1988) 'Constructing emotions: weaving emotions from memories', *British Journal of Social Psychology* 27: 19–34.

Kitzinger, C. (1986) 'Introducing and developing Q as a feminist method: a study of accounts of lesbianism', in S. Wilkinson (ed.) *Feminist Social Psychology*, Milton Keynes: Open University Press.

—— (1987) *The Social Construction of Lesbianism*, London: Sage.

Kline, P. (1981) *Fact and Fantasy in Freudian Theory*, London: Methuen.

Kohlberg, L. (1966) 'A cognitive-developmental analysis of children's sex-role concepts and attitudes', in E. Maccoby (ed.), *The Development of Sex Differences*, Stanford: Stanford University Press.

Kornbrot, D. (1987) 'Science and psychology degree performance', *Bulletin of the British Psychological Society* 40: 409–17.

Krieger, S. (1982) 'Identity and lesbian community: recent social science literature', *Signs* 8: 91–108.

Kristeva, J. (1980) *Desire in Language*, Oxford: Blackwell.

Kuhn, A. and Wolpe, A. (1982) *Women's Pictures*, London: Routledge & Kegan Paul.

Lacan, J. (1977) *Ecrits*, London: Tavistock.

Ladner, J. (1979) 'Growing up Black', in J. Williams (ed.) *Psychology of Women: Selected Readings*, New York: Norton.

Lakoff, R. (1975) *Language and Woman's Place*, New York: Harper & Row.

Lawrence, E. (1983) 'Just plain common sense: the "roots" of racism', in Centre for Contemporary Cultural Studies (ed.) *The Empire Strikes Back*, London: Hutchinson.

Laws, J. (1975) 'The psychology of tokenism: an analysis', *Sex Roles* 1: 51–67.

Lipschitz, S. (1978) '"The personal is political": the problem of feminist therapy', *m/f* 2: 22–31.

Lloyd, B. and Archer, J. (1976) *Exploring Sex Differences*, London: Academic Press.

Locksley, A. and Colten, M. (1979) 'Psychological androgyny: a case of mistaken identity?', *Journal of Personality and Social Psychology* 37: 1017–31.

Loewenstein, S., Bloch, E., Campion, J., Epstein, J., Gale, P. and Salvatore, M. (1985) 'A study of satisfactions and stresses of single women in midlife', in J. Williams (ed.) *Psychology of Women: Selected Readings*, New York: Norton.

Lorenz, K. (1978) *King Solomon's Ring*, London: Methuen.

Lott, B. (1985) 'The potential enrichment of social/personality psychology through feminist research and vice versa', *American Psychologist* 40: 155–64.

Luria, Z. (1986) 'A methodological critique', *Signs* 11: 316–21.

McAdoo, H. (ed.) (1981) *Black Families*, New York: Sage.

McAdoo, H. and J. (eds) (1985) *Black Children*, New York: Sage.

McClelland, D., Atkinson, J., Clark, R. and Lowell, E. (1953) *The Achievement Motive*, New York: Appleton-Century-Crofts.

Maccoby, E. and Jacklin, C. (1974) *The Psychology of Sex Differences*, Stanford: Stanford University Press.

—— (1980) 'Sex differences in aggression: a rejoinder and reprise', *Child Development* 51: 964–80.

McRobbie, A. and McCabe, T. (eds) (1981) *Feminism For Girls*, London: Routledge & Kegan Paul.

McRobbie, A. and Nava, M. (eds) (1984) *Gender and Generation*, London: Macmillan.

Major, R. (ed.) (1982) *Affranchissement: du transfert et de la lettre*, Paris: Editions Confrontation.

Mannion, K. (1981) 'Psychology and the lesbian', in S. Cox (ed.) *Female Psychology*, Chicago: Science Research Associates.

Marcus, L. (1987) '"Enough about you, let's talk about me"': recent autobiographical writing', *New Formations* 1: 77–94.

Marshall, J. (1984) *Women Managers*, London: Wiley.

Martinez, J. (ed.) (1984) *Chicano Psychology*, New York, Academic Press.

Maslow, A. and Chiang, H-M. (1977) 'Laboratory in self-knowledge', in H-M Chiang and A. Maslow (eds) *The Healthy Personality*, New York: Van Nostrand.

Mayall, B. and Petrie, P. (1983) *Childminding and Day Nurseries: What Kind of Care?* London: Heinemann Education.

Maynard Smith, J. (1978) *The Evolution of Sex*, Cambridge: Cambridge University Press.

Metz, C. (1982) *The Imaginary Signifier*, Bloomington, Ind.: University of Indiana Press.

Miller, G. (1969) 'Psychology as a means of promoting human welfare', *American Psychologist* 24: 1063–75.

Miller, J. (1976) *Towards a New Psychology of Women*, Boston: Beacon.

Mitchell, J. (1974) *Psychoanalysis and Feminism*, Harmondsworth: Penguin.

Moi, T. (1985) *Sexual/Textual Politics*, London: Methuen.

—— (1987) *French Feminist Thought*, Oxford: Blackwell.

Money, J. and Ehrhardt, A. (1972) *Man and Woman, Boy and Girl*, New York: Johns Hopkins University Press.

Montagu, A. (ed.) (1980) *Sociobiology Examined*, Milton Keynes: Open University Press.

Moraga, C. and Anzaldúa, G. (eds) (1981) *This Bridge Called My Back*, Watertown, Mass.: Persephone Press.

Morgan. K. and Ayim, M. (1984) 'Comment on Bem's "Gender schema theory and its implications for child development: raising gender-aschematic children in a gender-schematic society"', *Signs* 10: 188–96.

Morgan, R. (1970) *Sisterhood is Powerful*, London: Vintage.

Morin, S. (1977) 'Heterosexual bias in psychological research on lesbianism and male homosexuality', *American Psychologist* 32: 629–37.

Murgatroyd, S. (1982) 'Counselling and the BPS: a caution', *Bulletin of the British Psychological Society* 35: 452–3.

National Women at Work Conference (1987) 'Announcement', *Bulletin of the British Psychological Society* 40: 398.

New. C. and David, M. (1985) *For the Children's Sake*, Harmondsworth: Penguin.

Newman, C. (1985) Unpublished letter to the proposers of a Psychology of Women Section.

Nicholson, J. (1984) *Men And Women: How Different Are They?*, Oxford: Oxford University Press.

Nobles, W. (1980) 'African foundations for Black psychology', in R. Jones (ed.) *Black Psychology*, New York: Harper & Row.

Norris, C. (1987) *Derrida*, London: Fontana.

Nye, R. (1982) *Three Psychologists*, Monterey, California: Brooks/Cole.

Oakley, A. (1972) *Sex, Gender and Society*, London: Temple Smith.

O'Connell, A. and Russo, N. (eds) (1983) *Models of Achievement: Reflections of Eminent Women in Psychology*, New York: Columbia University Press.

Orbach, S. (1978) *Fat is a Feminist Issue*, London: Hamlyn.

Orbach, S. and Eichenbaum, L. (1987) *Bittersweet*, London: Twentieth Century Hutchinson.

Over, R. (1984) 'Career prospects within British universities', *Bulletin of the British Psychological Society* 37: 150–2.

Parker, I. (1989) *The Crisis in Modern Social Psychology and How to End It*, London: Routledge.

Parker, I. and Shotter, J. (eds) (1989) *Deconstructing Social Psychology*, London: Macmillan.

Parlee, M. (1975) 'Psychology of women', *Signs* 1: 119–38.

—— (1979) 'Psychology and women', *Signs* 5: 121–33.

—— (1981) 'Appropriate control groups in feminist research', *Psychology of Women Quarterly* 5: 637–44.

Parmar, P. (1983) 'Gender, race and class: Asian women in resistance', in Centre for Contemporary Cultural Studies (ed.) *The Empire Strikes Back*, London: Hutchinson.

Pečjak, V. (1985) 'Micro and macrouses of psychology', in R. Dias-Guerrero (ed.) *Cross-Cultural and National Studies in Social Psychology*, Amsterdam: Elsevier.

Phillips, A. (1987) *Divided Loyalties*, London: Virago.

Phoenix, A. (1987) 'The social context of motherhood', Women in Psychology Conference, Brunel University.

Piaget, J. (1950) *The Moral Judgement of the Child*, London: Routledge & Kegan Paul.

Pleck, J. (1975) 'Masculinity-femininity: current and alternative paradigms', *Sex Roles* 1: 161–78.

Pleck, J. and Sawyer, J. (eds) (1974) *Men and Masculinity*, London: Spectrum.

Ponse, B. (1978) *Identities in the Lesbian World*, Westport, Connecticut: Greenwood Press.

Potter, J. and Wetherell, M. (1987) *Social Psychology and Discourse Analysis*, London: Sage.

Pratt, M. (1986) 'Scratches on the face of the country', in H. Gates (ed.) *'Race', Writing and Difference*, Oxford: Oxford University Press.

Rachlin, H. (1980) *Behaviorism in Everyday Life*, New York: Prentice Hall.

Radicalesbians (1973) 'Woman-identified women', in P. Brown (ed.) *Radical Psychology*, New York: Harper & Row.

Rainwater, L. (1972) 'Some aspects of lower class sexual behavior', in J. Bardwick (ed.) *Readings on the Psychology of Women*, New York: Harper & Row.

Ramirez, M. (1985) 'Combining modernism and traditionalism', in R. Dias-Guerrero (ed.) *Cross-Cultural and National Studies in Social Psychology*, Amsterdam: Elsevier.

Reicher, S. (1984a) 'The St Paul's riot: an explanation of the limits of crowd action in terms of a social identity model', *European Journal of Social Psychology* 14: 1–21.

—— (1984b) 'St Paul's: a study in the limits of crowd behaviour', in J. Murphy *et al.* (eds) *Dialogues and Debates in Social Psychology*, London: Erlbaum.

Rich, A. (1977) *Of Woman Born*, London: Virago.

—— (1980) 'Compulsory heterosexuality and lesbian existence', *Signs* 5: 631–60.

Riley, D. (1978) 'Developmental psychology, biology and marxism', *Ideology and Consciousness* 4: 73–982.

—— (1983) *War in the Nursery*, London: Virago.

—— (1987) 'Does sex have a history? "Women" and feminism', *New Formations* 1: 35–46.

Rioch, M. (1983) 'Autobiographical sketch', in A. O'Connell and N. Russo (eds) *Models of Achievement: Reflections of Eminent Women in Psychology*, New York: Columbia University Press.

Roazen, P. (1985) *Helene Deutsch*, New York: Anchor.

Rodgers Rose, F. (1980) *The Black Woman*, New York: Sage.

Rodrigues, A. (1985) 'Social-psychological characteristics of Brazilians', in R. Dias-Guerrero (ed.) *Cross-Cultural and National Studies in Social Psychology*, Amsterdam: Elsevier.

Rose, J. (1978) '"Dora" – fragment of an analysis', *m/f* 2: 5–21.

Rose, N. (1985) *The Psychological Complex*, London: Routledge & Kegan Paul.

Rowbotham, S. (1973) *Woman's Consciousness, Man's World*, Harmondsworth: Penguin.

Rowbotham, S., Segal, L. and Wainwright, H. (1979) *Beyond the Fragments*, London: Merlin.

Russ, J. (1985) *The Female Man*, London: Women's Press.

Russo, N. (1982) 'Psychology of women: analysis of the faculty and courses of an emerging field', *Psychology of Women Quarterly* 7: 18–31.

Ryan, M. (1982) *Marxism and Deconstruction*, Baltimore: Johns Hopkins University Press.

Said, E. (1984) *The World and Text, and the Critic*, London: Faber.

Sandoval, C. (1984) 'Comment on Krieger's "Identity and lesbian community: recent social science literature"', *Signs* 9: 725–9.

Sayers, J. (1982) *Biological Politics*, London: Tavistock.

—— (1986) *Sexual Contradictions*, London: Tavistock.

Schor, N. (1981) 'Female paranoia: the case for psychoanalytic feminist criticism', *Yale French Studies* 62: 204–19.

Segal, L. (1987) *Is the Future Female?*, London: Virago.

Shainess, N. (1970) 'A psychiatrist's view: images of woman – past and present, overt and obscured', in R. Morgan, (ed.) *Sisterhood is Powerful*, London: Vintage.

Sharpe, S. (1984) *Double Identity*, Harmondsworth: Penguin.

—— (1987) *Falling in Love*, London: Virago.

Sherfey, M. (1970) 'A theory on female sexuality', in R. Morgan (ed.) *Sisterhood is Powerful*, London: Vintage.

Sherif, C. (1977) 'Bias in psychology', in J. Sherman and E. Beck (eds) *The Prism of Sex*, Madison: University of Wisconsin Press.

Sherman, J. (1971) *On the Psychology of Women*, Springfield: Charles Thomas.

Skinner, B. (1953) *Science and Human Behavior*, New York: Macmillan.

Smith, B. (1983) *Home Girls*, New York: Kitchen Table Press.

Smith, B. and Smith B. (1981) 'Across the kitchen table: a sister-to-sister dialogue', in C. Moraga and G. Anzaldúa (eds) *This Bridge Called My Back*, Watertown, Mass.: Persephone Press.

Smith, P. and Casbolt, D. (1984) 'Sixth formers and psychology: fifteen years on', *Bulletin of the British Psychological Society* 37: 334–7.

Sophie, J. (1985–6) 'A critical examination of lesbian identity development', *Journal of Homosexuality* 12 (2): 39–51.

Spector Person, E. (1980) 'Sexuality as the mainstay of identity: psychoanalytic perspectives', *Signs* 5: 605–30.

Spender, D. (1980) *Man Made Language*, London: Routledge & Kegan Paul.

—— (1982) *Women of Ideas (And What Men Have Done To Them)*, London: Routledge & Kegan Paul.

Spivak, G. (1981) 'French texts/American contexts', *Yale French Studies* 62: 154–84.

—— (1986) 'Three women's texts and a critique of imperialism', in H. Gates (ed.) *'Race', Writing and Difference*, Oxford: Oxford University Press.

—— (1987) *In Other Worlds*, New York: Routledge, Chapman & Hall.

Squire, C. (1989a) 'Crisis what crisis?', in I. Parker and J. Shotter (eds) *Deconstructing Social Psychology*, London: Macmillan.

—— (1989b') 'Feminism as antipsychology', in E. Burman (ed.) *The Practice of Psychology by Feminists*, Milton Keynes: Open University Press.

Stack, C. (1975) *All Our Kin*, New York: Harper & Row.

—— (1986) 'The culture of gender: women and men of color', *Signs*, 11: 321–4.

Stanley, L. and Wise, S. (1983) *Breaking Out*, London: Routledge & Kegan Paul.

Steedman, C. (1986) *Landscape for a Good Woman*, London, Virago.

Stoller, R. (1974) *Splitting*, London: International Psychoanalytic Library.

Tajfel, H. (1979) (ed.) *Differentiation Between Social Groups*, London: Academic Press.

Thaxton, L. and Jaret, C. (1985) 'Singers and stereotypes: the images of female recording artists', *Sociological Inquiry* 55 (3): 239–63.

Tieger, T. (1980) 'On the biological basis of sex differences in aggression', *Child Development* 51: 943–63.

Tittle, C. (1986) 'Gender research and education', *American Psychologist* 41: 1161–8.

Tizard, B. (1987) *The Care of Young Children*, London: Thomas Coram Research Institute.

Tizard, B. and Hughes, M. (1984) *Young Children Learning*, London: Fontana.

Toulmin, S. (1953) *Philosophy of Science*, London: Hutchinson University Library.

Trivers, R. (1972) 'Parental investment and sexual selection', in B. Campbell (ed.) *Sexual Selection and the Descent of Man*, London: Heinemann.

Tronto, J. (1987) 'Beyond gender differences to a theory of care', *Signs* 12: 644–63.

Turkle, S. (1979) *Psychoanalytic Politics*, London: Burnett.

—— (1984) *The Second Self*, London: Granada.

Unger, R. (1979) *Female and Male: Psychological Perspectives*, New York: Harper & Row.

—— (1982) 'Advocacy versus scholarship revisited: issues in the psychology of women', *Psychology of Women Quarterly* 7: 5–17.

—— (1983) 'Through the looking glass: no wonderland yet! The reciprocal relation between methodology and models of reality', *Psychology of Women Quarterly* 8: 9–32.

Urwin, C. (1985) 'Constructing motherhood: the persuasion of normal development', in C. Steedman, C. Urwin and V. Walkerdine (eds) *Language, Gender and Childhood*, London: Routledge & Kegan Paul.

Ussher, J. (1987) 'Racist propaganda', *Bulletin of the British Psychological Society* 40: 302.

—— (1989) *Psychology and the Female Body*, London: Routledge.

Walker, A. (1984) *In Search of our Mothers' Gardens*, London: Women's Press.

Walker, L. (1984) 'Sex differences in the development of moral reasoning: a critical review', *Child Development* 55: 677–91.

—— (1986) 'Sex differences in the development of moral reasoning: a response to Baumrind', *Child Development* 57: 522–6.

Walkerdine, V. (1986) 'Video replay: families, films and fantasy', in V. Burgin and C. Kaplan (eds) *Formations of Fantasy*, London: Methuen.

Walkerdine, V. and Lucey, H. (1989) *Democracy in the Kitchen*, London: Virago.

Wallston, B. (1981) 'What are the questions in the psychology of women? A feminist approach', *Psychology of Women Quarterly* 5: 597–617.

Walsh, M. (1985) 'Academic professional women organising for change: the struggle in psychology', *Journal of Social Issues* 41 (4): 17–28.

Watters, A. (1986) 'Heterosexual bias in psychological research on lesbianism and male homosexuality (1979–1983), utilising the bibliographical and taxonomic system of Morin (1977)', *Journal of Homosexuality* 13: 35–58.

Weisstein, N. (1973) 'Kind, Kuche, Kirche as scientific law: psychology constructs the female', in P. Brown (ed.) *Radical Psychology*, New York: Harper Colophon.

Weston, P. and Mednick, M. (1972) 'Race, social class, and the motive to avoid success in women', in J. Bardwick (ed.) *Readings in the Psychology of Women*, New York: Harper & Row.

Wetherell, M., Stiven, H. and Potter, J. (1987) 'Unequal egalitarianism', *British Journal of Social Psychology* 26: 59–71.

Whyte, L. (1967) *The Unconscious Before Freud*, London: Tavistock.

Wilkinson, S. (ed.) (1986a) *Feminist Social Psychology*, Milton Keynes: Open University Press.

—— (1986b) 'Diversity and community in feminist research', in S. Wilkinson (ed.) *Feminist Social Psychology*, Milton Keynes: Open University Press.

—— (1988) 'New Psychology of Women Section', *The Psychologist* 1: 7.

Williams, J. (ed.) (1979, 1985). *Psychology of Women: Selected Readings*, New York: Norton.

Wilson, A. (1978) *Finding A Voice*, London: Virago.

Wilson, E. (1981) 'Psychoanalysis: psychic law and order', *Feminist Review* 8: 63–78.

Wine, J. (1985) 'Models of human functioning: a feminist perspective', *International Journal of Women's Studies* 8: 183–92.

Wittig, M. (1985) 'Dilemmas in the psychology of gender', *American Psychologist* 40: 800–11.

Women in Psychology (1985) *Unpublished reports on proposals for a Psychology of Women Section in the British Psychological Society.*

Wong, N. (1981) 'In search of the self as hero', in C. Moraga and G. Anzaldúa (eds) *This Bridge Called My Back*, Watertown, Mass.: Persephone Press.

Woolf, V. (1979) *Women and Writing*, London: Women's Press.

Wyatt, T. (1987) 'How habitat leads to mothercare', *New Scientist* 1581: 50–3.

Zimmerman, B. (1984) 'Lesbian personal narratives', *Signs* 9: 663–82.

Index

Greeno and Maccoby 50
Greer 12, 23, 28, 29, 49, 65-6, 84,
    87, 90, 98
Griffen 37
Griffin, C. 37
Griffin, S. 79

Habermas 95
Halpern 67-8
Hanfmann 59
Harari and Peters 27, 38
Hardyment 116
Harlow 61
Hartnett and Shimmen 10
Haug 84, 90
Heilbrun, A. 54
Heilbrun, C. 52
Henle 7, 12
Henley 17, 58, 68-70, 90,
    112
Henriques *et al*. 9, 95, 107-10,
    116, 121
Herriot 10
Hirst and Wooley 66
Hiscock 45
Hobson, D. 104
Hobson, S. 21
Hollway 74, 108-10
Hooks 17
Horner 30-1, 34-5
Horney 98-9
Horney 66
humanist psychology 47-8, 53-5,
    72-4, 87-92
Humphrey and Haward 13
Hussain 108
Hutt 61, 63

individually-oriented methods 45-6,
    51
interactionism 63, 68
interdisciplinarity 3, 8, 35, 38, 40,
    58, 68, 103, 113
interview method 43, 49-51, 53-4,
    56, 87-8, 115
Irigaray 102, 106

Johnson 42

Jones *et al*. 54

Kaplan, A. and Sedney 52, 54, 56
Kaplan, C. 78, 103, 106
Kimmell 14
Kippax *et al*. 87
Kitzinger 40, 51, 117
Klein 15, 66, 97
Kline 96
Kohlberg 15, 26, 28, 29, 31, 64,
    71-2, 92
Kohut 99
Kristeva 102, 106

Lacan 100-6, 108, 110
Ladner 42, 70, 116-20
Lakoff 49, 105
Lampl-de-Groot 15
language 3, 39, 48-9, 67, 85-6, 89,
    100-6, 110, 112-15, 117-23
Laws 13, 14, 15
Lévi-Strauss 101
Lipschitz 100
Locksley and Colten 53, 55
Lorde 87
Lorenz 62-3
Lott 68, 87, 92, 115
Loewenstein *et al*. 37

McClelland *et al*. 26
Maccoby and Jacklin 15, 26, 28,
    29, 31, 33, 34, 50, 69, 99
Mack Brunswick 15
Marcuse 98
Marshall 85
Maslow 10, 47, 73
Maslow and Chiang 47-8
mathematical ability 30, 36, 45,
    67
menstruation 65, 85
metaphor 120-1
Miller, G. 81
Miller, J. 79-80, 86, 89-93
Mitchell 100, 102, 106
Moi 102
Money and Ehrhardt 64
Moraga and Anzaldúa 87
moral reasoning 29, 31-2, 37, 52-6,